Endorseme

Scandalous Love breaks all the rules! This could be a headline for the Jerusalem Times. How could a perfect God choose to associate with wretched people like that?!! Zack Wechsler is helping us see where the love of God and religious practice part ways. This journey through the gospel helps the reader to see how powerfully our Father's love impacts the lives of human beings. This book is a focus on the dramatically practical ways God loves us. It is also a template for how we then receive and impart this love to others. I highly recommend this book to those who are wanting to see and apply the enormous and unpredictable love of the Father every day of their life.

Danny Silk
President of Loving on Purpose,
Author of *Keep Your Love On* and *Unpunishable*

Zack Wechsler is an artist, a wordsmith, a storyteller, and a ferociously joyful lover of God. He has a rare grace for being culturally edgy and timelessly relevant at the same time. In Zack's public ministry, and in the words of this book, I can't help but think of Jesus, equally comfortable teaching on a hillside or a synagogue, weaving profound wisdom into engaging tales of wayfaring strangers and wandering sons, all to unveil a new covenant of unimaginable goodness. The ability to simplify profound theology is a gift of grace and whether you're new to faith or a seasoned minister, this book will serve as a new covenant discipleship manual that will give you a fresh perspective on the scandalous love of God.

Bill Vanderbush
Author/Speaker

Scandalous Love is a book committed to creating opportunity for the reader to gain a deeper understanding of God's love. The love of God is the most fundamental tenet of the gospel, yet so many people lack true understanding of its depth and ability to transform. In this book, Zack Wechsler provides multiple on-ramps for the reader to encounter and explore a fresh revelation of the unconditional and unwavering love of God! Read this book and get a fresh experience with the love of God!

Christa Smith
Author of *Singled Out in a Couples World*,
Speaker, Sean & Christa Smith Ministries

God has given Zack Wechsler a very profound, weighty revelation of the love of God and the gospel of Jesus Christ! Very few people I know carry it as deeply as he does. Zack is a true apostle of God's love! I heard Zack preach about the woman at the well at a conference and my heart was inflamed and my eyes in tears because of God's unending and unwavering kindness. If you are longing for a deeper encounter and revelation of God's love for you, this book is a must! This book reveals and imparts the good news that Abba Father God has more than enough of his scandalous love just for you. It is abundantly overflowing; just surrender to it and BE LOVED by God!!!

Jason Chin
Author of *Love Says Go*,
Founder of Love Says Go Academy, Missionary to Europe

Zack Wechsler is a unique composite of characteristics. He fuses preacher, theologian, musician, comedian, pastor, worship leader, and author with 100 percent love. What makes *Scandalous Love* so powerful is the authentic love that flows from the heart of Zack to the reader. If we have ever needed an infusion of love, it's today. Our world is writhing in bias, bigotry, and unmitigated hatred. Zack Wechsler has given us an antidote to this poisonous hostility—God's scandalous love! This book is a timely tool to reach people with the love of God, and there is no one better to do it than Zack Wechsler.

Larry M. Titus
President of Kingdom Global Ministries

I strongly believe that the message of the Father's love is what the world needs more than anything today. *Scandalous Love* helps to bring clarity to that message. It is a clarion call, a beacon to help shine light on God's extravagant love that pierces every dark place in our lives.

Lonell Brinson Sr.
Senior Pastor, Redeeming Word
Christian Center International

In this book, Zack Wechsler invites you on an adventure where you discover that God intends to completely upend your concept of how he loves you! It's a journey that will never end, straight into his light that reveals how fiercely his love pursues you and how completely his love makes you whole. He is utterly relentless in his scandalous love that won't take no for an answer until you live in the freedom his Son died to provide for you.

Don't turn the last page of this book without allowing the rich contents within these pages to work in you and transform you from the inside out. It's time to know Jesus as you are known — as the object of his relentless pursuit, fueled on by his scandalous love!

Dr. Roberts Liardon
Author of *God's Generals* series

This book is the core message that God is speaking to every person's heart. This is where healing to our problems lies. Do not let this opportunity pass you by. Zack's new book will bring you closer to Father God and flood your heart with love for him.

Dr. Harold R. Eberle
President of Worldcast Ministries and Publishing

When I saw the title I knew something good was coming. Zack Wechsler does not live in a confined area. He is constantly pushing the boundaries to seek and find God's true nature and to declare it with fire and love. *Scandalous Love* is a must book for all who have questions concerning God's great affection for them. Zack masterfully weaves life stories in with pertinent Scripture and profound revelation in a way that makes this such a joyous read. A perfect gift for your own heart as well as others.

Chris DuPré
Pastor, worship leader, and author of *The Wild Love of God*

Zack Wechsler paints a beautiful picture of the unrelenting love of God as he offers a deeper and refreshing look into familiar passages of Scripture. Allow the healing words in this book to lead to joy, gratitude, and wonder as you encounter scandalous Love.

Shae Bynes
Author and Kingdom Business Strategist

In *Scandalous Love*, Zack Wechsler confronts the perception that God is distant, controlling, and punishing. He affirms that, from the very beginning, God's interaction with us has always been driven by love, scandalous love. As the reader journeys through the life of Jesus and the history of the church, it becomes obvious that every word and action of the Savior is filled with the proof of his Father's love toward us. You can try to run from this love; however, you will find yourself running right into it. As you read this book you will feel his grip and never want to escape it. The great news is that scandalous love does not have to remain in the stories of the Scriptures or the testimonies of the past. Even today, the Father's love is changing and impacting the lives of those who receive it.

Chris Ball
President of Elim Fellowship

This book is an eye-opener, a must-read! It is contagious and inspirational. Zack's book reveals the heart of God and pierces the darkness with Love. It is a tool to reach people who are still in doubt of who their creator is. I hope you can meet Zack in person; he carries the tangible love of God and reading this book will put you on a journey of experiencing that love. *Scandalous Love* is a love story about God's unfailing love for you. I recommend Zack and this powerful book.

Dr. Gershom Sikaala
Author, speaker, pastor, humanitarian

Zack does an incredible job of removing the darkness of religion and shining a bright light on the heart of Christ. The heart that beats with a scandalous love for you and me. Read this book, give it away, and then read it again to see how much the Trinity loves and enjoys you!

Zach Maldonado
Speaker, pastor, and bestselling author of *Jesus Is Better*

"Never judge a book by its cover" is perfect for this book that encapsulates for its reader a message from the heart of God. It is a spiritual love note that has no judgments or religious limitations, but speaks to all people, saved, unsaved, and seeking. Zack, you provided essential tools for the reader to walk through a journey of understanding that God is LOVE. Thank you for unfolding his acts of forgiveness and restoration through the plan that he has for us. This book is a masterpiece for the Now Revival that is in our land. Thank you, Zack, for birthing such a revelatory message to the world.

Bishop Clinton House
Pastor, Mountaintop Faith Ministries

"Love people for who they are, right where they are, and they will become who they are supposed to be." That phrase right in the middle of Zack Wechsler's new book, *Scandalous Love*, is why

Jesus' ministry was so loved by the ordinary person and hated by the religious. He was a friend of sinners and people felt truly safe in his presence. Jesus spoke to the Son in people and did not focus on the sin in them, for his scandalous love chose to see what others could not. Zack does an excellent job in this book, painting a picture of the Father's heart revealed through Christ Jesus. This heart picture shows God's true character, which is light, life, and love. I wholeheartedly encourage all to read this book, meditate on its message, and ultimately demonstrate what this scandalous love looks like in our everyday lives, and to give others as much grace as we all need ourselves.

Jamie Englehart
Author, speaker, bishop of C.I.M. Network of churches and ministries

Zack Wechsler has beautifully written a book that challenges our paradigms of thinking around two words: scandalous and love. This is more than just a book, it is a clarion call to the heart of the Father who is love. Zack has written this book in a way that enables you to feel the tangible love of God being made manifest through each page. I don't recall reading another that has caused me to cry like this. The presence of heaven is all over this book. Readers will find themselves moved to tears from their own scandalous pain, as they are being healed by God's greater scandalous love. *Scandalous Love* is an invitation to step into a life unlocked by the redeeming power of the love of God.

Dr. Tony Robinson
Conference speaker, consultant, life coach

Scandalous Love is theologically rich and an empowering message that reveals the heart of the Father. This book is a fire starter! It causes you to come alive to your true identity and lead others into the same victorious lifestyle. It is a privilege to see

Zack Wechsler lead his church communities through the very message and heart of this book.

Steve Hogan
Pastor, Business Leader

To say that this book will be life changing for many who read it would be an incredible understatement. I have been close with Zack for many years, and I can say without hesitation that the words he has penned in this treasure are in fact the words that he believes. *Scandalous Love* will take you on a journey into the love of God, so much that you will never see Him in the same way — and you will never doubt his love for you again. This is a must-read for every new believer and anyone who is stuck in the "God looks kinda like Zeus" camp. Life changing!

Chris Ritchie
Senior Leader, Encounter Church Vegas

With a deep commitment to Scripture, Zack encourages us to take a fresh look at an ancient truth, and shows us through real life testimonies, just how much our lives can change when we encounter this scandalous love.

Michael T. Leyde
Pastor, worship leader, songwriter—The Pursuit NW

ZACKARY D. WECHSLER

SCANDALOUS

LOVE

REDISCOVERING THE **AUTHENTIC GOSPEL** THAT **REPELS**
THE RELIGIOUS AND **ATTRACTS** THE **BROKENHEARTED**

HIGHERLIFE
PUBLISHING & MARKETING

Scandalous Love
Published by Higher Life Development Services Inc.
PO Box 623307
Oviedo, Florida 32762
www.ahigherlife.com
Copyright © 2022 Zackary Wechsler
ISBN: 978-1-954533-90-5 (Paperback)
978-1-954533-91-2 (ebook)
Library of Congress Control Number: 2022904672

Scripture quotations marked (AMP) are taken from the *Amplified Bible*, copyright © 2015 by The Lockman Foundation, La Habra, CA. Used by permission.

Scripture quotations marked (ESV) are taken from The Holy Bible, English Standard Version * (ESV*), copyright © 2001 by Crossway, a publishing ministry of Good News Publishers. Used by permission.

Scripture quotations marked (MSG) are taken from *The Message*. Copyright © 1993, 1994, 1995, 1996, 2000, 2001, 2002. Used by permission of NavPress Publishing Group.

Scripture quotations marked (NASB) are taken from the NEW AMERICAN STANDARD BIBLE*, copyright © 1960, 1962, 1963, 1968, 1971, 1972, 1973, 1975, 1977, 1995 by The Lockman Foundation. Used by permission.

Scripture quotations marked (NIV) are taken from the Holy Bible, New International Version*, NIV*. Copyright © 1973, 1978, 1984, 2011 by Biblica, Inc.™ Used by permission of Zondervan. All rights reserved worldwide. www.zondervan.com The "NIV" and "New International Version" are trademarks registered in the United States Patent and Trademark Office by Biblica, Inc.™

Scripture quotations marked (NKJV) are taken from the New King James Version, copyright © 1982 by Thomas Nelson Inc. Used by permission. All rights reserved.

Scripture quotations marked (NLT) are taken from the Holy Bible, New Living Translation, copyright © 1996, 2004, 2007, 2013 by Tyndale House Foundation. Used by permission of Tyndale House Publishers, Inc., Carol Stream, Illinois 60188. All rights reserved.

Scripture quotations marked (TLB) are taken from The Living Bible, copyright © 1971 by Tyndale House Publishers, Wheaton, Illinois 60187. All rights reserved.

Scripture quotations marked (TPT) are taken from The Passion Translation* 2020 by Passion & Fire Ministries, Inc. Used by permission.

Printed in the United States of America.

10 9 8 7 6 5 4 3 2 1

CONTENTS

Dedication   xv

Introduction   1

CHAPTER ONE Scandalous Love   3

CHAPTER TWO Afraid of the Light   11

CHAPTER THREE Original Christian Gospel   25

CHAPTER FOUR Illegal Discount   41

CHAPTER FIVE A Thirst for Love   53

CHAPTER SIX The Jealous Lover   71

CHAPTER SEVEN It's God's Fault!   87

CHAPTER EIGHT Lies, Damn Lies, and Insignificance   105

CHAPTER NINE Half Dead and Bleeding Out   117

CHAPTER TEN The Abba of Jesus   129

SPECIAL THANKS

I am thankful for the many people who cheered me on to write this book.

First to my beloved wife, Rachelle. You are my #1 cheerleader. Thank you for always getting on my case to complete what I start and always telling me who I really am. I love you. To my kids, who literally spoke life into me when I was discouraged. I'm so proud of all of you. I love you with all my heart. And all five of you are my favorite.

I'm thankful to my dad and mom for always loving me so well as parents and believing in me. Mom, your love and support have always been a huge comfort through rough times. You're the best mom in the entire world. Dad, your tenacity to fight, to love fiercely, and always be positive has shaped me as a father and a man. If I could be half the man you are, I could raise 10,000 sons. I love you, Pops.

Thanks to all those that have poured into me and have influenced me over the years. Thank you to my church fam, and the Encounter Movement. Let's change the world!

DEDICATION

I would like to dedicate this book to a spiritual father, Larry M. Titus. Without your love and affirmation, I'm not sure I would be where I am in ministry today. Thank you for loving me, believing in me, for always answering your phone, and investing in me. It's very evident that your love for me loudly resounds the heart of God the Father.

LYRICS FOR THE HEART

I Was Made
I'm stunned by your beauty
Astounded by your grace
That you would include me
and now we're face to face
and now we're face to face
You encase your love around me
I hear your words of life
I have been invited
to look into your eyes
to look into your eyes
I was made to be loved by you
I was made for loving you

ZACK AND SARAH WECHSLER

INTRODUCTION

FOR MANY YEARS NOW it's been stirring in my heart to write a book about what I believe is the most important thing for all of humanity to know and experience—the outrageous love of God. I have seen the love of God transform the hardest of hearts and heal the most broken of souls, including my own.

This book is not regurgitating stuff that sounds nice, nor is it an attempt to appeal to some trendy intellectual need. Rather, it is about the ancient Christian gospel that transforms lives. We will be going much deeper into what the gospel is and what it means to us.

Now, when I say *gospel*, it's possible you have heard a version of the story of Jesus, or met some guy on a street corner yelling at people in the name of God and calling that the gospel. Well, I'm hoping this book will undo the misconceptions of what the gospel is. This book is a revelation of the love of God. The gospel of Jesus Christ is the story of that love.

The vast beauty of the gospel can't be unveiled in one book, but we will embark on a journey together to unfold a greater understanding of the gospel and how it is interwoven into the scandalous love of God. This is a truth I have worked through over the years, studying theology, pastoring, being pastored, and simply living the Christian life.

I pray that as you read these pages, you will receive the heavenly healing oil that flows from them. These words come from a heart that has been touched and transformed by the love of God. I long to see others encounter the depths of that same love.

I give you fair warning: you're about to discover the *Scandalous Love* of God.

CHAPTER ONE

SCANDALOUS LOVE

GOD'S LOVE IS SCANDALOUS! Not merely amazing, unconditional or grand, but scandalous! We're talking eye-popping, heart-racing, headline-grabbing, neighbors-talking scandalous! And the good news? Nothing spreads like scandal. After all, the world is full of scandals and scandalous people. What would the internet be without them? It may seem sacrilegious to ascribe scandal to God's love, but in fact, the gospel of Jesus is full of scandal. Just ask the Pharisees.

Scandal to us in the modern world may not seem appropriate. Jesus is portrayed as a nice guy, a kind, compassionate teacher of goodness. Where's the scandal in that? A scandal is front-page news that stirs people's pots and sets tongues a-wagging. That doesn't sound like the felt-board Sunday school Jesus, does it? Imagine little Johnny coming home from vacation Bible school and telling his mother: "Jesus was scandalous." Mommy will be looking for another church.

The truth is, Jesus was revolutionary; he caused scandal just by his presence. He was a walking controversy from the moment he was born. Imagine a band of swarthy shepherds running through town in the middle of the night, reeking of sheep and raving about this angel, a savior and where can they find a manger. *Sure, guys. There are only 10,000 mangers in Bethlehem. By the way, who's watching your flock?* I'm surprised they weren't arrested before reaching the swaddled babe.

Jesus' arrival terrified King Herod so badly that the despot went to desperate lengths trying to destroy him. (Spoiler alert: Herod failed.)

Things didn't get much better with age. When Jesus was twelve, during his family's annual pilgrimage to Jerusalem—most likely part of a caravan—Jesus missed the ride home, driving his parents to search frantically for three days! They finally found him in the temple, surrounded by teachers, and they were incredulous!

> *When Joseph and Mary saw Him, they were bewildered; and His mother said to Him, "Son, why have You treated us this way? Behold, your father and I have been anxiously looking for You!"*
>
> *And He said to them, "Why is it that you were looking for Me? Did you not know that I had to be in My Father's house?"*
>
> LUKE 2:48-49 NASB

The fact is, Jesus scandalized people everywhere he went, with as great an intensity as he drew them. The same Spirit of God attracted or repelled the populace and especially those whose religion meant more than life itself.

> **The same Spirit of God attracted or repelled the populace and especially those whose religion meant more than life itself.**

In Matthew 13, we find one of those crowd-enraging, scandalous moments in Jesus' life. He was in his hometown of Galilee and the people "took offense" at the things he said. Take a look:

> *When He had come to His own country, He taught them in their synagogue, so that they were astonished and said,*

"Where did this Man get this wisdom and these mighty works? Is this not the carpenter's son? Is not His mother called Mary? And His brothers James, Joses, Simon, and Judas? And His sisters, are they not all with us? Where then did this Man get all these things?" So they were offended at Him.

MATTHEW 13:54-57 NKJV

In this example, his own townies were scandalized by his words and presence! Think of it: all Jesus had to do was show up! Jesus was teaching and it says they were astonished by his authority and wisdom and wondered openly how Jesus could be so legit. After all, they knew his mom and dad. Ironically, they were so familiar with Jesus that they missed the God stuff. Like the poet Chaucer observed: "Familiarity breeds contempt." Instead of believing in the content of Jesus' message, they chose to reject the mes-

> **It's hard to hang on to the Jesus we grew up with when the real one shows up in love and power!**

senger. This wasn't simply Joseph's son, the little kid learning to pound nails and level a main-bearing beam. This was the Son of God, and his wisdom, power and love was just too much for his people to handle. Can you imagine their thoughts? *No way. It couldn't be true. It doesn't seem right. Who does he think he is? I remember when he was in short pants (a short toga?).*

The same thing happens today. We all have an image of Jesus, usually from childhood, mostly favorable but maybe not. And it's hard to hang on to the Jesus we grew up with when the real one shows up in love and power! It's scandalous to challenge our childhood Jesus. Who is this guy . . . really? Vile sinners wanted to hang out. He healed all that he touched. And the religious wanted to throw him off a cliff? So scandalous!

Scandal was nothing new to the Jews, living as they were under the oppressive yoke of Rome. The Greek word is *skandalízō*, and surely it was used often during Jesus' ministry. The word *scandal* appears over twenty times in the Greek Old Testament (Septuagint), and fifteen times in the New Testament. Scandal is a transliteration of the Greek word σκάνδαλον (pronounced *skandalon*). This word in many contexts means: "a trap or a snare or what might cause someone to stumble or fall into sin." In some Scriptures it's applied to Jesus himself and the gospel.

> *But we preach Christ crucified, to the Jews <u>a stumbling block</u> and to the Greeks foolishness,*
> 1 CORINTHIANS 1:23 NKJV

> *As it is written:*

> *"Behold, I lay in Zion a stumbling stone and rock of offense, And whoever believes on Him will not be put to shame."*
> ROMANS 9:33 NKJV (ALSO SEE 1 PETER 2:8)

> *And I, brethren, if I still preach circumcision, why do I still suffer persecution? Then <u>the offense of the cross</u> has ceased.*
> GALATIANS 5:11 NKJV (EMPHASIS ADDED)

We all know of modern-day scandals. I'm sure we've been involved in some scandalous things. Yet even the darkest scandals and the most sinful situations can't compare to the scandalous, outrageous, jaw-dropping love displayed in Jesus Christ. It is more than a love of comfort; it is a love of upheaval, revolution, violently arresting the designs of sin.

Consider a typical scandal. Perhaps a husband and a wife both commit adultery. Take it further: one of them becomes a prostitute while still married to their spouse. Making matters worse, they are pillars in the church. Sounds pretty scandalous, right? The love of God wouldn't touch that scene in a million years. Or would it?

One of the metaphors of God's love for his people is found in the Old Testament. The prophet Hosea was told by God to marry a prostitute—not someone who ended up cheating on him, but a life-long prostitute, one sold into bondage to the brothels. Hosea was to welcome and love her, joining himself to her in the marriage covenant. And after she married him, despite Hosea's ardent love, what did she do? She eventually went back to prostitution. Of course.

This is where the story gets really scandalous. God told Hosea to keep chasing after her, even if that meant searching for her in the brothels and buying her freedom . . . more than once. That's much more scandalous than the scandal of the sin itself. Can you hear the locals? *That fool. He should have known what he was marrying. She'll be the ruin of him. See what love gets you?*

> There is no true forgiveness without love, and no love without forgiveness. The more profound the love, the greater the forgiveness.

What the scandalized populace failed to understand is the radical nature of God's love.

> *Then the Lord said to me [Hosea], "Go and love your wife again, even though she commits adultery with another lover. This will illustrate that the Lord still loves Israel, even though the people have turned to other gods and love to worship them."*
>
> HOSEA 3:1 NLT

There is no true forgiveness without love, and no love without forgiveness. The more profound the love, the greater the forgiveness. In later chapters, we will talk more about this type of love story—a love that seeks us in our mess. Prepare to be overwhelmed, shaken to the core by the fierce, redeeming love of God.

This is the scandalous love God displayed through the life of Jesus. While we were in utter darkness, sold to sin, in debt with our very lives, Jesus redeemed us and brought us into union with himself, forgiving us, redeeming us, healing us and giving us life. This is why Jesus himself was such a scandal. The religious leaders hated him while the crowds found healing in his presence. It sounded too good to be true, but it was truth itself. If the gospel is not offensive to us—if the gospel is not this big mountain in front of us that doesn't make sense—maybe we've never encountered it before.

What's even more scandalous is that this love is not just for a few special people. All are welcomed and invited to receive. Yes, the most scandalous of sinners and self-righteous of religious zealots. All of humanity is called to come and drink of the living water that Jesus gives.

The Spirit and the bride say, "Come." Let anyone who hears this say, "Come." Let anyone who is thirsty come. Let anyone who desires drink freely from the water of life.

REVELATION 22:17 NLT

These words of John are not referring to the return of Jesus in all of his glory. This is an evangelistic appeal to the broken and lost sinners to come and freely drink.

Outside the city are the dogs—the sorcerers, the sexually immoral, the murderers, the idol worshipers, and all who love to live a lie.

REVELATION 22:15 NLT

Yeah . . . even these guys.

Wow! So scandalous. None so undeserving as those listed in that verse, but they, along with all of humanity, are welcome to come and drink of the pure waters of salvation. Why? Because God's love is scandalous to the most religious and the worst of sinners. Scandalous to the Pharisees because Jesus revealed a love that superseded the legal system and religious treadmills they inhabited. Scandalous to the sinners because it just seemed too good to be true—finding forgiveness, healing, and life from none other than God himself!

- Would it be scandalous if an IRS employee, one who had been robbing from people for years, suddenly decided to confess, and then he doesn't even do prison time for it?
- Would it be scandalous if a woman caught in adultery was allowed to go free without any sort of public condemnation?
- Would it be scandalous if a convicted criminal were completely pardoned and given a new lease on life?
- Would it be scandalous if a godly man married a prostitute, and every time she left him, he went to the brothel to buy her back as his wife?

Absolutely this would be scandalous. Yet this is what we see in the Bible in the life of Jesus as he reveals the heart of the Father towards broken humanity.

Let's take a journey through Scripture and some profound real-life testimonies of God's scandalous love.

With your heart postured to receive, my prayer is joined with the Apostle Paul's prayer for the Ephesian church:

> *May you experience the love of Christ, though it is too great to understand fully. Then you will be made complete with all the fullness of life and power that comes from God.*
> EPHESIANS 3:19 NLT

Oh, how deep and wide is the love of God! God's love is scandalous to the soul that has been seized by religion and shocking to the worst of sinners. I hope you're ready to discover the depths of the scandalous love of God!

Reflection, Discussion, and Prayer

1. In what ways has God's scandalous love challenged the religious attitudes in your heart?

2. Ponder on how shocking it would be for God to forgive our sins. Reflect on what he has forgiven in your life.

3. Consider the example of Hosea pursuing his wife even as she continued being unfaithful. Give some examples of God pursuing you when you were unfaithful to him.

CHAPTER TWO

AFRAID OF THE LIGHT

I have come into the world as a light, so that no one who believes in me should stay in darkness.

JOHN 12:46 NIV

BEING SCARED OF THE dark is a real thing, especially for kids. My youngest daughter, Laylah, was an exception, however. For some reason, she wasn't afraid of things that terrified normal kids. In Nevada, we had a house near a large greenbelt surrounded by desert. The area was haunted by nocturnal creatures: bobcats, coyotes, politicians, and homeless people. Terrifying, right? Well, not to my five-year-old, redheaded princess. As we strolled the verdant greenbelt in the cool of evening, she'd bolt for the wild without a care. No wonder we called her "brave." She had zero fear of the pitch-black night! I was more scared than she was, but it was fear for her . . . of course.

The good news is most of us outgrow our fear of the dark. What I find strange, however, is that many of us are afraid of the light—the light of God's scandalous love. Let's take a closer look.

Blinded by the Light

In Acts 9, we read of a religious zealot "breathing out murderous threats" on his way to Damascus to stamp out a heretical insurrection among the churches under his authority. His name was Saul, and he was in a bad mood.

His attitude lightened, however, when he was accosted by God on the road to perdition.

Suddenly a light from heaven flashed around him. He fell to the ground and heard a voice say to him, "Saul, Saul, why do you persecute me?"

ACTS 9:3-4 NIV

Turns out the people he thought were heretics were actually experiencing heavenly revelation. And this religious leader named Jesus, who Saul thought was inciting this spiritual insurrection, was actually from God. Indeed . . . he *was* God in the flesh, and Saul needed to get on the right side of him.

> **The light didn't blind him; it revealed his true spiritual condition.**

He fell to the ground and heard a voice say to him, "Saul, Saul, why do you persecute me?"

"Who are you, Lord?" Saul asked.

"I am Jesus, whom you are persecuting," he replied. "Now get up and go into the city, and you will be told what you must do."

The men traveling with Saul stood there speechless; they heard the sound but did not see anyone. Saul got up from the ground, but when he opened his eyes he could see nothing. So they led him by the hand into Damascus. For three days he was blind, and did not eat or drink anything.

ACTS 9:1-9 NIV

Saul got up blind, yet the light didn't blind him; it revealed his true spiritual condition.

Talk about a wakeup call! It stopped him in his tracks, but it didn't end there. Saul yielded to this fiery love of Jesus, and the light brought him healing and salvation.

Then Ananias went to the house and entered it. Placing his hands on Saul, he said, "Brother Saul, the Lord—Jesus, who appeared to you on the road as you were coming here—has sent me so that you may see again and be filled with the Holy Spirit."

Immediately, something like scales fell from Saul's eyes, and he could see again. He got up and was baptized, and after taking some food, he regained his strength.

ACTS 9:17-19 NIV

Saul had been possessed by deep darkness; his entire worldview was distorted. Although he could see in the flesh, he was blinded by his religious zeal. Earlier, he had a part in killing a young man named Stephen, the first Christian martyr (ref. Acts 7). Yet after one encounter with Jesus, he went from sightless religious zealot to humble saint of the Christian faith!

Darkness hides our true reality; the light of God exposes it. No wonder we're afraid of the light! Our true spiritual condition is darkness!

Jesus then said, "I came into the world to bring everything into the clear light of day, making all the distinctions clear, so that those who have never seen will see, and those who have made a great pretense of seeing will be exposed as blind."

JOHN 9:39 MSG

Jesus exposes us, bringing everything into the clear light of

13

day. Some of us welcome this. Others recoil from it. That's why some see and others are blind. This is what happened to Saul, at least temporarily. Had Saul chosen not to yield to the light of Jesus, he may have remained blind. Instead, he came into the light and received healing. Amazingly, he ended up writing most of the New Testament by the light of that encounter.

Next time we are tempted to ask why God doesn't simply zap our enemies and be done with them, remember Jesus' pursuit of Saul down his dark road!

The Plank in Our Eye

First and foremost, this darkness—which comes from our spiritual blindness, our sin and our fallen condition—affects everything. It completely distorts reality, including how we view God. You see, in this darkness, we form inaccurate images of God and we react to them.

Have you ever woken at night and seen things that weren't real? When morning comes, what you thought were tangible threats were fantasies borne of darkness. Shadows can look quite different than reality. As a kid, I saw the dark shape of a monster against my bedroom wall, but in reality, it was a harmless little dog. Well, the same can happen spiritually.

> Because we are focused on the shadow instead of the light, we see a distorted image of God, a warped shape of who he really is.

Because we are focused on the shadow instead of the light, we see a distorted image of God, a warped shape of who he really is.

Religious zeal is part of our darkened condition. We create doctrines that support our image of a vengeful God ready to wipe us out! Living in the shadows teaches us to be terrified of God. But in the light of Jesus, we see clearly!

Therefore do not let anyone judge you by what you eat or drink, or with regard to a religious festival, a New Moon celebration or a Sabbath day. These are a shadow of the things that were to come; the reality, however, is found in Christ.

COLOSSIANS 2:16-17 NIV

The shadow in this verse is the Old Covenant that veiled God's full identity. Jesus, through the New Covenant, revealed the perfect image of the Father. As a Jewish scholar, Saul did not think he was spiritually blind. Then again, he didn't know his view of God was about to radically change. In his rage, he thought he was doing God's work, but the light of Jesus exposed his true state. He was delusional, consumed by hate, burning with a distorted image.

Whether we are holding onto sins or fueled by blind zeal, as we come into the light, we must allow God to kick down our idols, slaughter our sacred cows, and destroy impressions of him formed in our darkened imaginations.

Most of us understand our fallen state, knowing we are in need of saving grace. Yet we have become acclimated to running from the light as we cope with darkness, trying to coexist with both realms. We keep our pain, sin, and wounds—yes, even our church wounds—hidden in darkness, thinking it best to lock them away. But embracing our sin never leads to freedom. Ironically, we perpetuate the very damage that occurred because of our darkness.

The truth is, we all have baggage we could bring into the light, but it's hard sometimes, isn't it? *God is going to get mad and wipe us out!* Oh really? As if he doesn't know already. (He sees us in the shower; that should tell us something.) But . . . we're afraid. So we nurse our petty offenses, past sins, pain, and heartaches, and everything gets worse. Sometimes, we hide our brokenness because we fear what others might think. We put on a fake smile when we are screaming inside. The most tragic conversation in Christianity goes like this:

"How are you?"

"Fine. And you?"

"Oh, fine."

Uh huh . . .

When I was young, hide and seek was only fun with the lights off. (Maybe that's where my daughter gets it!) One time, I was playing in pitch-black darkness with friends, and a few of us got hurt. We were running around and it sort of turned into blind tag. We ran into doors, walls, each other. (I learned why football players wear helmets.) The same thing happens when we live in darkness; we are not designed to live without light. We play this silly game of hide and seek with God as if he doesn't know how to find us. Thinking we are protecting ourselves, we prolong our brokenness.

> **We play this silly game of hide and seek with God as if he doesn't know how to find us. Thinking we are protecting ourselves, we prolong our brokenness.**

The good news is, there is a better way.

> *If we claim that we experience a shared life with him and continue to stumble around in the dark, we're obviously lying through our teeth—we're not living what we claim. But if we walk in the light, God himself being the light, we also experience a shared life with one another, as the sacrificed blood of Jesus, God's Son, purges all our sin.*
>
> 1 JOHN 1:6-7 MSG

See the Kingdom

In John 3, the great teacher Nicodemus came to Jesus under

cover of darkness, fearing to be seen with this revolutionary rabbi. Clearly, if Nicodemus' religious buddies saw him conversing with Jesus, his reputation and their religious order would suffer ruin. How often do we hide from God in our religiosity? Even our zeal to do good can be another form of darkness. Let's see how Jesus handled this clandestine meeting.

> *This man [Nicodemus] came to Jesus by night and said to Him, "Rabbi, we know that You are a teacher come from God; for no one can do these signs that You do unless God is with him."*
>
> *Jesus answered and said to him, "Most assuredly, I say to you, unless one is born again, he cannot see the kingdom of God."*
>
> JOHN 3:2-3 NKJV

After this eminent scholar missed the point, having confused Jesus' words with something merely natural, he asked the pivotal question:

> *Nicodemus said to Him, "How can a man be born when he is old? Can he enter a second time into his mother's womb and be born?"*
>
> *Jesus answered, "Most assuredly, I say to you, unless one is born of water and the Spirit, he cannot enter the kingdom of God."*
>
> JOHN 3:5 NKJV

I'm sure this seemed revolutionary, even scandalous, to the befuddled Jewish leader. Born again? Huh? Starting from scratch? The embryonic emergence of a lifeform. Learning to think and talk, walk and run? Growing up all over again? Mystifying, to say the least.

Of course, this is exactly what happens. God's kingdom reign brings loving order to our lives, and with it healing, freedom, restoration, peace, and life as he designed it. Sounds good to me! I'll take some of that! Yet if we look closer at what Jesus said in verse 3, we see that we don't *enter* into the kingdom reign of God unless we first *see* the kingdom of God.

It's simple, really. Light is required for us to see as God intended us to see. Nicodemus came to Jesus by night, and Jesus told him he can't see the kingdom of God because it requires being born of the Spirit. It's the Holy Spirit that floods us with the light of God's love, opening our eyes to see the kingdom of God.

Consider Paul's prayer to the church of Ephesus:

> *I pray that the light of God will illuminate the eyes of your imagination, flooding you with light, until you experience the full revelation of the hope of his calling—that is, the wealth of God's glorious inheritances that he finds in us, his holy ones!*
>
> Ephesians 1:18 TPT

As the Spirit breathes upon us, we see God's kingdom and live as he created us to live. If we want freedom and healing, we must welcome the light of God's love, bringing our whole being into this kingdom of light.

Contrary to popular belief, our need to be born again is not simply so we can spend eternity with Jesus. Of course, that's amazing. Thank God for an eternity with him. But God doesn't just breathe upon us once and give us life for our final destination. He continues to breathe in our lives, day by day, moment by moment! Salvation is not just a guarantee of heaven; it is also an ongoing reality.

*The path of the righteous is like the morning sun, shining
ever brighter till the full light of day.*

PROVERBS 4:18 NIV

Jesus has saved us from a very real death, taking on our sins in
his broken body. He defeated the enemy of our souls—the devil—
and he also saves us from this present darkness, which is much
darker than we can imagine.

*For he has rescued us from the dominion of darkness and
brought us into the kingdom of the Son he loves.*

COLOSSIANS 1:13 NIV

Jesus never denied the reality of this domain of darkness; he
simply shined in the midst of it and brought us out of it. Jesus
loves to shine in the darkest places. Wherever there are broken
sinners, Jesus is there, wanting to pour out his love on them.
Even in the deep parts we keep hidden, even in the places only
he knows about, Jesus wants to heal us and shed his love into
every wound.

During Jesus' ministry on earth, he especially cared for the
rejected and the afflicted. He loved broken people, and his acceptance is what they needed to be whole. That's what light does: it
heals and sets free. True healing and freedom can only come as
we yield to him and receive his light. He sets us free from our
sin and pain, our self-righteousness and religious zeal! There is
no reason to fear the light. Adam and Eve hid from God, but it
didn't last long. Sadly, many are still trapped under the domain
of darkness thinking they're protected. They're not. They're only
protracted.

Feeling Trapped in the Darkness

I'm convinced there is more theology in a game of hide and seek
than in many Sunday sermons. As a child, I learned to find the

best hiding spots. (Sometimes, I hid so well, I couldn't find my way out.) The key is to remain quiet. When you hear the seeker getting close, freeze! *Don't dare move a muscle.* It's like hearing a noise late at night; everything stops. We hold our breath, fearing something bad if we're found out. (That's why people in horror movies don't run away from the bad guy.)

We do the same thing in our darkness, holding to our fear, our pain, our sin. The key here, however, is to be found. No matter how much junk we think we have, no matter how bad it appears, we can't freeze up. Who are we afraid of? The God of light? He's come to free us! The key to healing and freedom is being transparent in the light. Quit hiding; get found!

Jesus' love reaches the deepest pit, freeing both honest sinner and hypocritical saint. We all face blindness. God calls us into his light and freedom.

You Are Not Your Pain

Some wounds are so severe, they leave deep scars with lasting pain. They don't heal easily, but they do heal. Hear me: Your pain is real. What is real is not always right. You are *not* your pain.

Whether you are wrapped in darkness or running and hiding, you need to know that God is gentle. He doesn't turn the light on at 100 percent. He reveals himself gradually within our mess and gently lifts us into his loving arms. Scandalous doesn't mean abrupt. The love of God leads us into wholeness. There is no dark place he can't shed his love. No matter how deeply we might feel trapped, we are never beyond healing and freedom in Jesus. No one is beyond his forgiving grace, mercy, or the wholeness that God wants to bring to us all. This saving grace is through Jesus and is available to all of

> **Your pain is real. What is real is not always right. You are not your pain.**

humanity. We need only to trust and yield to the light of his love! There's nowhere else to go; we might as well turn to him. Consider our opening verse again, this time in a new light.

It's impossible to disappear from you or to ask the darkness to hide me, for your presence is everywhere, bringing light into my night.

PSALM 139:11 TPT

Open Up and Let the Light In

Maybe you, like many others, have tried repeatedly to find wholeness in conferences, self-help books, counseling, deliverance, or the shoulder of a friend, and found nothing works. Something helps for a time, but the pain creeps back to sabotage our self-worth, our relationships, and our spiritual lives. Yes, there is a process to healing, but if we still feel stuck in darkness, it's likely we have yet to discover God's scandalous love. Without God's love, we act like we are not in pain, we have it all together, but we're hiding a mess. It's the discovery of love that gives us the courage to let the light shine in every area of our lives. If I know I'm loved, I'll submit to cleansing and receive healing.

For you were once darkness, but now you are light in the Lord. Live as children of light.

EPHESIANS 5:8 NIV

Notice the subtle phrasing here. Paul tells the people of God they were once darkness, but now they are light in the Lord! Not that they are *in* light; rather, that they *are* light. This is profound. If we are running from light, and we are light, we are running from ourselves—our true selves in Christ.

There is healing and wholeness for you in Jesus. Regardless of who or what happened, how long ago or how recently . . .

21

regardless of all of the factors involved, there is nothing that can separate us from the love of God.

For I am convinced that neither death nor life, neither angels nor demons, neither the present nor the future, nor any powers, neither height nor depth, nor anything else in all creation, will be able to separate us from the love of God that is in Christ Jesus our Lord.

ROMANS 8:38-39 NIV

There was a time when I was broken over some bad choices and ugly circumstances, and I sank into depression. I walked in darkness and felt I had no light in my life. Emerging from this morass seemed impossible. Then I put on some worship music, and a beautiful song called *Open Up, Let the Light In*, by Steffany Gretzinger, lit up my life.

The song begins delicately with a soft piano and stringed instruments. It's like someone approaching your pain and softly taking your hand. The only lyric of the song is: "Open up, let the light in." Consumed by my hurt, I sensed the love of God pouring into my wounds. So simple yet so powerful. I began weeping. I didn't have to earn healing or be worthy of love. I simply had to open up and let the light in. My soul was raised out of the dark cloud.

> **His light doesn't condemn us; rather, it draws us into freedom. Yes, the light exposes our flaws, but it heals our pain.**

It started when God said, "Light up the darkness!" and our lives filled up with light as we saw and understood God in the face of Christ, all bright and beautiful.

2 CORINTHIANS 4:6 MSG

When we discover who God is, we can't help but run fearlessly into the light. His love is the sun melting away the ice and dirty snow of our past—the mistakes, pain, sin, and distortion that warp our image of God. Let us soak in the warm sun and flourish as we were designed to! God is light!

This, in essence, is the message we heard from Christ and are passing on to you: God is light, pure light; there's not a trace of darkness in him.

1 JOHN 1:5 MSG

Forget your religious reputation. Don't fear God's light. His love shines in the deep caverns of our souls. We are treasure to him. His light doesn't condemn us; rather, it draws us into freedom. Yes, the light exposes our flaws, but it heals our pain.

The light has come and his name is Jesus. Let that glorious light shine in and through you. No more hiding in the shadows; no more lurking in shame. It's time to walk in the life-giving light of Jesus.

Then Jesus spoke to them again, saying, "I am the light of the world. He who follows Me shall not walk in darkness, but have the light of life."

JOHN 8:12 NKJV

I pray you will open up and let the light in. Perhaps listen to *Open Up, Let the Light In* as you contemplate these truths. Or find your own song, the one you were meant to sing.

Reflection, Discussion, and Prayer

Consider the quote from this chapter: "Jesus exposes us, bringing everything in the clear light of day. Some of us welcome this. Others recoil from it."

1. How can you posture your heart so that you do not recoil from God's light?

2. God's light did not blind Saul; it revealed his true spiritual condition. Reflect on a time when the light of Jesus reached your darkness and pain.

3. Ask God to expose the lies you believed about him, those that hold you in darkness.

CHAPTER THREE

ORIGINAL CHRISTIAN GOSPEL

If your eye is pure, there will be sunshine in your soul. But if your eye is clouded with evil thoughts and desires, you are in deep spiritual darkness. And oh, how deep that darkness can be!

MATTHEW 6:22-23 TLB

A S A YOUNG BOY, my family and I attended mass twice a year. From this brief exposure, I acquired an image of God. He was a grumpy old man with a long white beard. His right hand held lightning rods like Zeus and, depending on his mood, he'd hurl them from heaven to zap anyone who dared to cross him. Thankfully, this image changed when I was six years old.

Someone gave me a prayer card bearing a picture of Jesus—a pleasant looking guy with soft brown hair, blue eyes and a warm smile. I liked it, so I taped it near the light switch in my room. Something about it made my room feel safer.

We lived in Denver, Colorado at the time, a place of volatile weather. Dark clouds, hail storms, and deep snow were normal. We could go for days without seeing the sun. When it finally broke through the clouds, the air became warm and alive.

One night, I had a vivid dream of Jesus. In the dream, the

heavens were obscured for days just like our weather. I was afraid, and then I saw Jesus standing before me. Suddenly, the clouds broke. His kind and humble face brought sunshine to my soul. I sensed such peace and love. All my fear vanished. He opened his arms and drew me closer.

Through the face of Jesus Christ, I saw God as he really is, not as a vengeful tyrant but powerfully loving. I now had a different fear for God; it was a holy awe, not a terrifying dread. As I looked into his eyes, I knew everything was going to be okay. He had what I needed. He was the answer. His love branded me so deeply, I've never lost that image.

Below the Surface

In the last chapter, we learned not to fear the light. In this chapter, we will understand that light. Fasten your spiritual seatbelts; we are about to properly define the gospel of Jesus through Scripture, Christian orthodoxy, and Jesus' true nature. No, this won't be a modern gospel that compromises everything and leaves us a mess. Instead, we will encounter ancient Christian truths, forgotten by many, that will set us free. So, let's delve deeper, throw open the veil and let the Son shine in!

There are deeper issues of darkness and sin; we don't always know their source or solution. So, how can we be whole? When someone is sick, we can relieve their pain but that doesn't cure them. Focusing on the symptoms can miss the root of the problem. Of course, we know that our brokenness is part of a world broken because of sin and the fall.

> *Therefore, just as through one man sin entered the world, and death through sin, and thus death spread to all men, because all sinned. . . .*
>
> ROMANS 5:12 NKJV

Yet our understanding of sin often remains at a surface level.

In defining sin, we cite what we see—the outward symptoms of a deeper issue. Consequently, we try to change the fruit instead of laying an axe to the root. The truth is, darkness is much deeper than we may realize. To get different fruit, we need a different tree.

The common understanding of sin is that of "missing the mark." A near-sighted archer comes to mind, one with a woeful assistant downrange with a quivering apple atop his head.

We often think of sin as breaking God's commandments through bad behavior. This incurs guilt, as informed by our conscience. *I shouldn't have stolen my sister's bike; I knew it was wrong.* But guilt doesn't get us deep heart cleansing.

In Greek, sin is the word *hamartia*. It means "to miss the mark, a fault, a failure, a sinful deed." The historical Christian church, however, understood sin as more than our deeds; it was a state of being. The difference is known as a juridical understanding of sin versus an ontological understanding of sin. Here's what it looks like.

> **Certain actions are indeed sinful, but sin is not merely what we do as fallen humans in a dark world. Sin is the darkness itself!**

When Adam and Eve sinned, they disobeyed God and ate the forbidden fruit. As bad as this was, the real tragedy was when they hid, turning their hearts away from love and communion with God.

A juridical understanding of sin—the action(s) of breaking God's law or missing the mark—applies to eating the forbidden fruit. Sin as a deed.

An ontological understanding of sin—our state of being, being corrupted by sin—applies to turning away from God. Sin as an attitude.

Of course, certain actions are indeed sinful, but sin is not merely what we do as fallen humans in a dark world. Sin is the darkness itself!

I like the way Fr. Arnold Bernstein defines sin in his book, *The Original Christian Gospel.*

Sin is the failure to realize life as love and communion, the failure to be whole, healthy and complete. It is the rejection of personal communion with God.

It shouldn't shock us that Adam and Eve hid as soon as they turned away from communion with God.

When they heard the sound of God strolling in the garden in the evening breeze, the Man and his Wife hid in the trees of the garden, hid from God. God called to the Man: "Where are you?"

GENESIS 3:8-9 MSG

Hiding was the symptom; broken fellowship was the root problem. No wonder they hid from God! Not only did they mess up, they became messed up. Sin is deeper than the symptoms. It's a disease that pollutes the world and corrupts mankind. Sin—in the form of shame—immediately distorted Adam and Eve's view of God. Sin is a spiritual sickness. When we are sick, we present symptoms, including pain. I don't know about you, but I don't want to just numb the pain. I want the disease healed!

> **Hiding was the symptom; broken fellowship was the root problem.**

Spiritual Big Pharma

Lacking a complete understanding of sin, Christian life has become a spiritual pharmaceutical industry. Our church gatherings, sermons, theology, even our relationships function on a surface level to assuage discomfort. Because we view sin as deeds and not a condition, we define holiness as conformity to a set of outward standards. Thus, as long as we fit the mold, we think everything's fine . . . when it's not.

Certainly we can be thankful for modern medicine for easing pain, yet we realize that pain management does not cure the core problem. Likewise, sin-management sermons and guilt-tripping do not convey a gospel that can cure, heal, and set every captive free . . . truly free.

So if the Son sets you free, you will be free indeed.

JOHN 8:36 NIV

Do you want to be whole? Free? Well then, it's time to leave this spiritual pharmaceutical industry. No, I don't mean forsake church and ignore anointed teaching. On the contrary, when we leave this fruitless cycle of temporary fixes, we can extract the maximum benefit from church gatherings and God's Word. The key is this: If I was sick and didn't know the real problem, I'd find a doctor with the proper skills. A good physician. Perhaps . . . *The Great Physician.* And I'd align with practitioners who knew how he operated.

Undercover Boss

Have you ever seen the show *Undercover Boss*? High-level corporate executives leave their lofty offices and secretly take low-level jobs within their companies to find out how things are really going. Well, that's what Jesus did when he was born of the virgin Mary. He became God incarnate (God made flesh) to save humanity, and he did so in unusual ways.

It was just before the Passover Festival. Jesus knew that the hour had come for him to leave this world and go to the

Father. Having loved his own who were in the world, he loved them to the end.

Jesus knew that the Father had put all things under his power, and that he had come from God and was returning to God; so he got up from the meal, took off his outer clothing, and wrapped a towel around his waist. After that, he poured water into a basin and began to wash his disciples' feet, drying them with the towel that was wrapped around him.

He came to Simon Peter, who said to him, "Lord, are you going to wash my feet?"

Jesus replied, "You do not realize now what I am doing, but later you will understand."

"No," said Peter, "you shall never wash my feet."

Jesus answered, "Unless I wash you, you have no part with me."

JOHN 13:1, 3-8 NIV

Jesus loved his disciples to the uttermost end. And on this holy night at the end of Passover, he showed his divine love by washing their feet. Now, this was a scandalous moment for the disciples! In the first century, only the lowest servants washed feet. Even for the disciples to wash their Rabbi's feet would have been inappropriate. Today in middle-eastern cultures, you don't even show

> **This "undercover boss" didn't just come to tell us how to be holy, but to lead us into holiness through his extreme humility, pouring out his divine love.**

the bottom of your feet, especially at an important meal with a special Rabbi—the Son of God.

Yet Jesus not only washed his subordinates' feet, he also told them to show this same love to one another. Wouldn't it be an honor to humbly wash the feet of a great man or woman of God? Or even more so, the very feet of Jesus? Who wouldn't sign up for that?! Think about it, though. This is God in the flesh washing human feet! Wow! Talk about a plot twist.

Jesus became human and assumed the lowest place to wash our filth. This "undercover boss" didn't just come to tell us how to be holy, but to lead us into holiness through his extreme humility, pouring out his divine love.

Jesus Assumed It All

The Word became flesh and made his dwelling among us. We have seen his glory, the glory of the one and only Son, who came from the Father, full of grace and truth.

JOHN 1:14 NIV

Jesus is the word that became flesh. He made his tabernacle among us, right in the middle of dark, hopeless, and sinful humanity. St. Gregory the Theologian, one of the early church fathers, put it this way:

What is not assumed is not redeemed. What he was, he laid aside; what he was not, he assumed. He takes upon himself the poverty of my flesh so that I may receive the riches of His divinity.

What does it mean for Jesus to *assume*? St. Gregory does not mean "to presume or suppose," but rather "to take on or accept something in its fullness." You see, Jesus fully took on (assumed) our humanity. Of course, Jesus was without sin, but he still assumed human flesh. He fully took on our brokenness and the disease of sin, entering our deepest darkness and lifting us out.

> *For God made the only one who did not know sin to become*
> *sin for us, so that we might become the righteousness of God*
> *through our union with him.*
>
> 2 CORINTHIANS 5:21 TPT

Jesus is the great physician, not only because he died on the cross, but because he lived fully human: the Son of God, the Son of Man.

> *But for you who revere my name, the sun of righteousness*
> *will rise with healing in its rays.*
>
> MALACHI 4:2 NIV

Jesus came as a healer. When you're sick and in pain, you don't need a judge, even though you've broken the law. You need a physician to make you whole. As Christians, we affirm that Jesus was fully God and fully human. This theology is the *hypostatic union*. Our redemption is not only in the finished work of the cross—that is a vital part of our redemption and the climax of the gospel story. But our redemption is also in the incarnation of God (becoming human) in the person of Jesus Christ. Of course, the price was paid for sickness and disease by the stripes Jesus bore on his back (ref. 1 Pet 2:24), but Jesus was the great healing doctor before the stripes and crucifixion. No wonder sinners sought his presence; it was a healing balm.

Jesus came into this world to fully take on our fallen humanity.

> *As Jesus was on his way, the crowds almost crushed him.*
> *And a woman was there who had been subject to bleeding*
> *for twelve years, but no one could heal her. She came up*

*behind him and touched the edge of his cloak, and immedi-
ately her bleeding stopped.*

LUKE 8:42-44 NIV

Jesus came into this world to fully take on our fallen humanity.
How? By joining his divinity to our fallen humanity in his very
incarnation. This is why the early Christians emphasized that Jesus was in
fact fully divine and fully human. We rarely hear the implications
of this taught in church today, but it's vital that we realize how
dark the darkness actually is and how deep Jesus went to free us.
This is *how* and *why* Jesus redeemed us.

Our salvation is not only in what Jesus did, but also *who he is.*
Jesus is our salvation, healing, and redemption. The life of Jesus
and all he endured in his incarnation was focused on our salvation! Starting in a manger, growing as a carpenter's son, baptized in the Jordan, fasting forty days, tempted in the wilderness,
opposed by the Jews, tortured by Rome, dying on a cross, and
resurrected on Easter morn. From virgin womb to empty tomb!
This was his very life. All . . . for . . . us.

When he fasted for forty days, he had no need to fast for himself. In his divinity, Jesus needed nothing. His fast was for our
healing, to equip us with grace to overcome. Consider what the
Coptic Orthodox Christian Church recites daily during lent:

Jesus Christ, fasted for us, forty days and forty nights.

It's all connected to our salvation.

*He understands humanity, for as a man, our magnificent
King-Priest was tempted in every way just as we are, and
conquered sin.*

HEB 4:15 TPT

Salvation is not just a singular event. Salvation is a person, and his name is Jesus. He was born to save us by becoming human. Let's look at two more powerful quotes from early church fathers that explain and affirm this even more.

You, the infinite, being God, did not consider equality with God a thing to be grasped, but emptied yourself and took the form of a servant, and blessed my nature in yourself, and fulfilled your law on my behalf.

ST. GREGORY OF NAZIANZUS - THE THEOLOGIAN
LITURGY "HOLY, HOLY, HOLY"

You have destroyed (death) by the life-giving manifestation of your only-begotten Son, our Lord, God, and Savior Jesus Christ.

LITURGY OF SAINT BASIL THE GREAT
PRAYER OF RECONCILIATION

God didn't come to weed-whack this mess that we have gotten ourselves into. He came to lay the axe to the roots of the disease of sin and death. He came to heal the land. He entered the fabric of our very DNA as a human, and in his glorious divinity brought us out of darkness, out of the deep spiritual sickness of sin woven into our broken hearts and souls. Through his life, he healed our fallen human nature. Jesus assumed it all! Look at this powerful quote from T.F. Torrance:

> **He entered the fabric of our very DNA as a human, and in his glorious divinity brought us out of darkness.**

In Jesus Christ the Son of God penetrated into the dark depths of our alienated, enslaved and distorted human existence, making it his own in order to heal, sanctify and renew it in himself throughout the whole course of his vicarious human life, death and resurrection and thus restore us to perfect loving union with God the Father.

Understanding that *to assume* means "to take on," let us again consider the profound words of St. Gregory of Nazianzus: "What is not assumed is not redeemed." Jesus took full responsibility for all of our sin, brokenness, and the disease that affects the entire world, and every human being in it.

When he served as a sacrifice for our sins, he solved the sin problem for good—not only ours, but the whole world's.

1 JOHN 2:2 MSG

If we are not living in the freedom and life of this healing, it's not because we need to strive more, but because we just don't believe that Jesus accomplished something that great for little ol' us. *It's too good to be true.* Well, here's the truth: The message of the gospel truly is scandalous. Let that shock you into a new spiritual reality.

The Real Gospel

Gospel: /ˈgäspəl/ *noun:* "good news."

So what is this *good news*? It's about God revealing his love to a broken world, not letting that world perish but redeeming us back to himself.

For God so loved the world that he gave his one and only Son, that whoever believes in him shall not perish but have eternal life.

JOHN 3:16 NIV

His love and light have come to us in our darkness and pain. He came to heal, forgive and free us from the reign of sin and death, to free us from our fallen selves. The gospel is the revelation of God in the person of Jesus. It is the gospel of the kingdom of God, the good news that a king was born, and not just any king but God himself. God became our nature so we could partake of his nature. He takes what is ours and gives what is His! In his humanity, he endured all things so we might partake of his divinity.

> *His divine power has given us everything we need for a godly life through our knowledge of him who called us by his own glory and goodness. Through these he has given us his very great and precious promises, so that through them you may participate in the divine nature, having escaped the corruption in the world caused by evil desires.*
>
> 2 PETER 1:3-4 NIV

I was once asked to define the gospel in a few words. Here it is.

The Gospel:

> *God assumed our fallen humanity,*
> *showed his love radically,*
> *revealing his divinity,*
> *gave his life willingly,*
> *restoring our true identity,*
> *that we might forever share in life*
> *Love and communion with the holy Trinity*

He revealed his divinity! When we look at Jesus, we see God's glorious face. We see who he really is!

> *It is only in and through Jesus Christ that man's eclipse of God can come to an end and he can emerge again out of darkness into light.*
>
> THOMAS F. TORRANCE, *THE ECLIPSE OF GOD*

God isn't the grumpy guy with lightning bolts correcting our behavior through fear of punishment. He actually became one of us to save us. God and man have been united forever in the incarnation. That's how much God loves you and me. That's how far he went!

These glorious truths that I'm sharing comprise the ancient orthodox Christian understanding of salvation. This is not new theology but rather a beautiful, neglected truth. It is the glorious light of the gospel of the Christian faith.

The Power of God

I want to close this chapter with a powerful testimony of how God rescued a young man from deep darkness!

There was a young man who grew up in an environment where crime and drugs were celebrated. His heroes were those who championed this lifestyle, so he took it on himself. He began to do drugs, then deal drugs, and he stole as a way of life.

> God and man have been united forever in the incarnation. That's how much God loves you and me. That's how far he went!

To cope with this dark life, he got involved with Hinduism, Taoism, Islam, and the like. This path led him into more deception, darkness, and bondage. At one point he actually thought he was God himself, although he could not escape his vices and bondage.

He believed he was destined to be a criminal and there was no way out. Fortunately, God had other ideas. One night, as he showered in preparation for another crime, the Holy Spirit touched him. It shook him to his core. God began cleansing him, delivering him from demonic strongholds. The young man exited the shower shrieking and fell on his knees before Jesus. The encounter lasted hours. God showed him the sin and darkness in the world, and the same in himself. It looked like grey smoke and resembled death itself. He was broken and undone as Jesus revealed a heart of love for him and the world. He wept for the brokenness he saw. Imagine someone preparing for a crime, now embodying Jesus' compassion for the broken world!

Despite being entrenched in false demonic religions, he felt compelled to pick up a Bible. Reading the words of Jesus, he realized everything God was telling him was confirmed in God's written Word. He stepped into the kitchen and turned on the light. At that very moment, Jesus spoke to his heart: "I have taken you out of darkness and brought you into my marvelous light."

That was the beginning of his new life in Christ! Later in his Bible reading, he felt Jesus speaking this Scripture straight to his heart:

> But you are God's chosen treasure—priests who are kings, a spiritual "nation" set apart as God's devoted ones. He called you out of darkness to experience his marvelous light, and now he claims you as his very own. He did this so that you would broadcast his glorious wonders throughout the world.

> 1 PETER 2:9 TPT

This young man's name is Sinclair. I'm honored to know Sinclair and to have him in my life. He is an awesome leader and evangelist for the gospel of the kingdom!

Reflection, Discussion, and Prayer

1. Sin is not just our actions; it is a spiritual disease. How does this truth help you walk in freedom, knowing that Jesus is our great physician?

2. What does it mean: "Jesus loved me to the uttermost," and "Jesus assumed it all"?

3. Ask God to reveal the religious prescriptions that have merely masked your pain instead of reaching the roots of your sin.

4. Based on the truth of the original Christian gospel, describe how God:

   • assumed our fallen humanity
   • showed his love radically
   • revealed his divinity
   • gave his life willingly
   • restored our true identity
   • that we might forever share in life, love, and communion with the holy Trinity.

CHAPTER FOUR

ILLEGAL DISCOUNT

But when the kindness and love of God our Savior appeared, he saved us, not because of righteous things we had done, but because of his mercy. He saved us through the washing of rebirth and renewal by the Holy Spirit, whom he poured out on us generously through Jesus Christ our Savior, so that, having been justified by his grace, we might become heirs having the hope of eternal life.

Titus 3:4-7 NIV

H OW SHOULD WE UNDERSTAND the gospel? I've heard so many confusing messages called *The Gospel.* They sound something like this:

You don't have worth, so Jesus died for you to give you worth. Now you're lovable so you don't have to experience hell forever because you believe in Jesus. Yay!

Or this:

It's not about you; it's only about Jesus. Empty yourself and be a cleansed vessel of nothing but Jesus. Your only value is in your nothing-ness.

Well, yeah, it's not *only* about us, but it's about us too. Did you know Jesus had you and me and all of humanity on his mind when his broken body was bleeding on the cross? I have some scandalous news for you: The cross was about you!

Your life is significant. You have worth! You are worth the life of God's Son.

Worthiness

The English language is tricky with words like *worth*, *worthy*, and *unworthy*. Not deserving something by merit is different than an intrinsic value. Jesus deserves our worship because he is worthy. He is God (intrinsic), and he paid our price (merit). He is the answer to the question posed in Revelation 5:2:

Who is worthy to break the seals and open the scroll?

This is why heaven sings in verse 12:

Worthy is the Lamb, who was slain,
to receive power and wealth and wisdom and strength
and honor and glory and praise!

God became flesh and revealed the love of the Father through his life and the finished work at Calvary because we are valuable. He looked at your life and all those throughout history, and although in our sin-condition we do not merit his grace, mercy, and love, intrinsically we are worth his life. The worth of anything is the price the buyer is willing to pay. Jesus paid the highest price possible: Himself . . . for you.

> The worth of anything is the price the buyer is willing to pay.

We cannot fully comprehend our value to the Father, Son, and Holy Spirit. I believe this to my core. Not understanding our worth is why we manage our symptoms instead of allowing his love to make us whole from our spiritual sickness. We are still trying to measure up, earn his love, and prove that his salvation was not in vain. We're trying to be good when all along, goodness has come to us, joined our lives and wants to restore us.

Here's a lie you need to let go of forever: *We were only valuable to God after we prayed the sinner's prayer.* No! Send this back to the pit of hell.

Yes, in one sense we have become even more valuable because he redeemed us—think of a cleaned vessel that was once corroded—but the idea that we obtained worth because of his saving act is wrong. In reality, we obtained salvation even while we had worth. The incarnation of Jesus Christ did not bestow our worth; it *proved* our worth.

Our lives change when we first encounter Jesus, and they change further when we actually believe God values us. Not just *believe* in theory. Sure, we say things like, "God loves me," but do we receive the truth of our value to him? I've known many Christians who thought God loved them but still feared going to hell if they skipped church. Deeply entrenched in our mind and hearts is a distorted view of *who God is* and *who we are* to God. We've got to get this straight.

I want to cut through these lies, these layers of religion, the false voices we assign to the Father: "Well, look at that little piece of trash. If it wasn't for the blood of Jesus, they'd be worthless."

These voices are not God. Yet they are rampant in our theology, and they show up in unexpected places. Martin Luther—the esteemed father of the protestant reformation—still thought people as manure covered in snow. As if God covers worthless manure with his mercy. Really? Yes, his mercy covers us, but that doesn't mean we are manure! Imagine a preacher today saying, "Look at your neighbor and say: 'You are snow-covered manure.'"

I have cleaned up dog manure in the winter, and guess what? Snow-covered manure is still manure! I have good news for you: You are not manure!

An Illegal Discount

A false sense of unworthiness even creeps into our prayers. I've heard people pray: "God, we are only valuable because of the cross."

Well, I've thought it through, searched the Scriptures and come to the opposite belief. We know we are loved and valuable *because* of the cross! The cross does not make us valuable; it proves we are valuable!

> **The cross does not make us valuable; it proves we are valuable!**

The finished work of Jesus is not only Jesus' death on the cross, burial, and resurrection, but also his very incarnation—God becoming flesh. Jesus changed everything, but that doesn't mean you weren't valuable before you were redeemed. Think about it: would he redeem something that didn't have value? God is smarter than that. Would he pay the immeasurable price for something that had no worth? No way!

Consider the parable of the lost coin. Did the lost coin have value before it was found? Of course it did. Nothing can change the worth with which God has imprinted you. When did he do that? Here:

> *Then God said, "Let us make mankind in our image, in our likeness."*
>
> GENESIS 1:26 NIV

You, me, mankind—we are made in the image and likeness of God. *The* God. The Godhead God. The Father, Son, and Holy Spirit God.

Yet many of us have allowed an illegal discount on our worth. I love a good deal when I'm shopping: 30%, 50% or even 75% off gets my attention. But what happens when we discount ourselves? We believe some poor theology that creates an illegal markdown of our souls. And that's wrong.

There are many reasons why this poverty mentality is

entrenched in our thinking. I will not attempt to take you through 2000 years of church history and theology; that is beyond the scope of this book. But I pray that you think these things through. Christians don't think enough today. As the Bible says: "Let my people *think*!" (OK, the Zack translation.)

It's easier to drink the religious Kool-Aid someone gives us because it's sweeter in the moment. It's easier than studying to show ourselves approved and actually thinking for ourselves. Let me tell you: the blood of Jesus—the wine of his abounding love—is so much greater than any Kool-Aid that religion can offer.

> The blood of Jesus—the wine of his abounding love—is so much greater than any Kool-Aid that religion can offer.

The Love of God

Layers of wrong thinking are evident in how we see and care for ourselves. A Christian of seventy years can still find their minds mired in the muck of lies. And yet the love of the Father's heart was so great (and still is) that Jesus:

- became human
- took on our human fallen nature
- never sinned
- shed his blood
- forgave our sins
- defeated the devil
- descended to the lower parts of the earth
- rose from the grave and overcame death

All because God loves us with a fiery relentless love. That is the gospel! That is the good news. Let me repeat this news to you:
God is not *mad* at you. He is actually mad *about* you!
His disposition toward you is love because that's who he is!

This is not some humanistic idea of an enabler God affirming every bad behavior or crazy idea dreamed up by fallen humanity. That would remake God in our image. Rather, this is truth borne out by historical Christian orthodoxy.

Whoever does not love does not know God, because God is love.

1 JOHN 4:8 NIV

God is Love. Easy to say, difficult to comprehend. How could God be love by nature? It's one thing to think God loves us, but God *being* love by nature is a challenging concept. God is not the god of religious mind (of any faith).

> **Love is not merely something God does; it is who he is. Love is his very essence. For God to stop loving us would require he cease to be God . . . and that's impossible.**

Since love requires relation to another, the truth that God is love can only be resolved in the doctrine of the Trinity. God is not solitary; he does not act alone. God is Father, Son, and Holy Spirit—three eternal, divine persons, one in essence. Notice the words at creation:

Let us make mankind in our image, in our likeness.

GENESIS 1:26 NIV

The word *our* implies more than one. In this case, it was the conversation of the very Godhead: Father, Son, and Holy Spirit.

"One essence in three persons. God is one and God is three: the Holy Trinity is a mystery of unity in diversity, and of diversity in unity. Father, Son, and Spirit are 'one in essence'" (Gregory of Nazianzus, Orations, 31, 14).

So, even before creation, God was hanging out with himself, Father, Son, and Holy Spirit, in perfect communion and love with one another. This is why our understanding of God as Trinity is so vastly different from other religions.

Love is not merely something God does; it is who he is. Love is his very essence. For God to stop loving us would require he cease to be God . . . and that's impossible.

The Divine Dance

Perichoresis is a Greek word the early church used to describe the relationship of the Trinity. It describes the ones without the loss of distinction. If that's too theological for you, *perichoresis* could also be defined as a "divine dance." Sounds kind of scandalous! Guess what's even more scandalous: You and I have been invited to this dance that occurs through the rhythms of his grace. (We will talk more of this later.)

The discovery of God's unending, fiery, amazing, and scandalous love is vital to all of us. It's not just a discovery of a feeling or an idea, but rather a revelation of who he is!

Your Real Price Tag

Before the universe was created—the billions of galaxies, stars, and planets—the Father, Son, and Holy Spirit had already put an adoption tag on you, regardless of any future creation. The Godhead put a price tag on you, and it read: PRICELESS, INVALUABLE, ACCEPTED, CHOSEN.

You better believe it! It's true!

> *Their God will save the day. He'll rescue them.*
> *They'll become like sheep, gentle and soft,*
> *Or like gemstones in a crown,*
> *catching all the colors of the sun.*
> *Then how they'll shine! shimmer! glow!*
> *the young men robust, the young women lovely!*
> ZECHARIAH 9:16-17 MSG

So, my very dear friends, don't get thrown off course. Every desirable and beneficial gift comes out of heaven. The gifts are rivers of light cascading down from the Father of Light. There is nothing deceitful in God, nothing two-faced, nothing fickle. He brought us to life using the true Word, showing us off as the crown of all his creatures.

JAMES 1:16-18 MSG

You are indeed the jewels of the crown; you are his prized possession, purchased with a price no one could ever number. Don't forget it!

Near the end of his earthly life, Jesus prayed that we would know and experience the reality of our value to him—that we are loved with the same love the Father has for him.

> **You are indeed the jewels of the crown; you are his prized possession, purchased with a price no one could ever number. Don't forget it!**

Father, I ask that you allow everyone that you have given to me to be with me where I am! Then they will see my full glory— the very splendor you have placed upon me because you have loved me even before the beginning of time.

I have revealed to them who you are and I will continue to make you even more real to them, so that they may experience the same endless love that you have for me, for your love will now live in them, even as I live in them!

JOHN 17:24, 26 TPT

Scandalous to the Religious

Years ago, during prayer at Sunday morning service, I said, "The cross does not make you valuable; it proves you're valuable!"

An angry man jumped up, turned sharply and stormed out of the church. At first, I was bothered that he would be offended at that statement. Really?! Why was it such a stumbling block to him? Was it really that scandalous that he would leave in the middle of service? Later, I got an angry call from him. "Where's that in the Bible, Pastor?!"

I was trying not to be aggressive, although I wanted desperately to lay some hands on that brother and perhaps pray for him . . . later. (I'm kidding, I think.) At that moment, my mind flooded with God's Word. Verse after verse to exemplify my point appeared in my mind. I decided to reply with one verse that I knew he would know (along with anyone who has ever watched sports). I said softly, slowly: "Umm. . . . How about John 3:16?"

He hung up.

I was perplexed. I mean, this guy had been a Christian for years, studied the Bible in some mainline charismatic denominations, and this offended him? Perhaps he was scandalized.

The gospel can be a bit offensive. The story of Jesus and what he accomplished is radical enough, but the reason he did it all is totally scandalous. It's because of his relentless, unfailing, and fiery love!

"God so loved . . ." (John 3:16). Go no further. Let these three words abolish every lie you have ever heard about the gospel. God doesn't love anything that is not valuable to him. That would be silly. Yet deep down, you may still feel as though you lack intrinsic value. Please allow God to change your heart, your thinking, and your life. You had value before his precious blood was shed, or he would not have shed it.

The Apostle Paul speaks of this love demonstrated because God loved and valued us *before* the cross.

For when the time was right, the Anointed One came and died to demonstrate his love for sinners who were entirely helpless, weak, and powerless to save themselves.

Now, who of us would dare to die for the sake of a wicked person? We can all understand if someone was willing to die for a truly noble person. But Christ proved God's passionate love for us by dying in our place while we were still lost and ungodly!

ROMANS 5:6-8 TPT

Christ proved his love by dying for us. His saving act speaks of our intrinsic value before the cross actually happened. When we yield our hearts and minds to the gospel, it exposes the self-righteous, religious lies that say we are worthless.

> **When we yield our hearts and minds to the gospel, it exposes the self-righteous, religious lies that say we are worthless.**

Scandalous to the Sinner

I was preaching a series on grace—you know, some catchy sermon series to fill the pews and entertain the saints. Ha! One Sunday after the message, we had a typical charismatic "altar call." To my surprise, the altar was flooded with people eager for God's love and forgiveness. Two of the people—a young man and woman—were weeping. *Wow! They are really encountering God's love!*

Later, I found out it was a pimp and a prostitute who were encountering God's grace! Interestingly, the angry man from the previous story who left in the middle of service, was related to the pimp and prostitute who received God's scandalous grace. The best part is, God loves us all, from the honest sinner to the hypocritical saint. We all need his love.

God's grace is amazing. As a pastor preaching on grace, I made a choice to believe that his grace is amazing. I could tell story after story of how I personally encountered God's love and how I'm still discovering the depths of his love! We will be discovering the depths of his love for all of eternity.

Look at what Jesus says in Matthew 6:26:

Look at the birds of the air, for they neither sow nor reap nor gather into barns; yet your heavenly Father feeds them. Are you not of more value than they?

Jesus asked a rhetorical question. "Are you not of more value than they?" Absolutely and unequivocally! Even in our flawed value system, what makes something valuable?

1. The price one is willing to pay for it. Well, that settles it! We can't even begin to know the price that Jesus paid for all of humanity. What a great price—his very life!
2. The uniqueness of it. Did you know that you are one of a kind? There is no one else like you on the planet. No one has your DNA and fingerprints. God knows every hair on your head. By the way, Jesus' statement was not about the great transcendent omniscience of God, but rather how his Father loves and cares for us.

Let's end this chapter with a powerful hymn: *The Love of God.* Take a moment and contemplate the sweet depths of his love. Read it slowly. Contemplate it. It wrecks me. May it do the same for you.

> *Could we with ink the ocean fill*
> *And were the skies of parchment made*
> *Were every stalk on earth a quill*
> *And every man a scribe by trade*
> *To write the love of God above*
> *Would drain the ocean dry*
> *Nor could the scroll contain the whole*
> *Though stretched from sky to sky.*
> FREDERICK MARTIN LEHMAN (1917)

Reflection, Discussion, and Prayer

1. When you discover that something you believed is wrong, how does that affect you?

2. "The cross does not make you valuable; it proves you're valuable." How does this statement change how you see yourself and the rest of humanity?

3. We have been invited into a divine dance with the Father, the Son, and the Holy Spirit. What is your response to that invitation?

4. Ask God to show you the times and reasons you did not see the price tag he put on your life.

CHAPTER FIVE

A THIRST FOR LOVE

For you reach into my heart.
With one flash of your eyes I am undone by your love,
my beloved, my equal, my bride.
You leave me breathless—
I am overcome
by merely a glance from your worshiping eyes,
for you have stolen my heart.
I am held hostage by your love
and by the graces of righteousness shining upon you.
How satisfying to me, my equal, my bride.
Your love is my finest wine—intoxicating and thrilling.
And your sweet, perfumed praises—so exotic, so pleasing.
SONG OF SONGS 4:9-10 TPT

BEING A FATHER OF five kids keeps me on my toes. They light up my world and help me understand the depths of the Father's love. I have three daughters, and they're all gorgeous. I do my best as a dad to give them affection and love and constantly tell them how beautiful they are. Sadly, not every daughter experiences that type of love from a father. My heart aches when I see the brokenness of a child who longs for the affection of a parent. That longing often becomes a gaping hole trying to fill itself—the classic pit of looking for love in all the wrong places.

When they were younger, if you asked my girls who they were

going to marry, they'd say, "I'm gonna marry my daddy." This melted my heart. There is something so sweet about being "daddy's little girl" or "momma's little boy." Of course, as my girls grew, they realized that marrying daddy was not a reality. And they're growing up so quickly! I want to freeze time, slow down, and cherish the present. (Would you take a moment and pray for me? They're becoming interested in dating. Lord have mercy . . . . especially on the boys they bring to the house.)

Of course, this is not everyone's experience as a child or a parent. Yet we are all meant to experience love, acceptance, affirmation, and affection. A parent's love for their children originates from God's heart; it's an expression of God's Trinitarian love to us all. It's how we're wired by our Creator. Both sons and daughters are made to be loved and accepted. Love, acceptance, affirmation, and affection are the rich soil in which our lives are meant to thrive and bear fruit.

> **We are all meant to experience love, acceptance, affirmation, and affection.**

I'm not a perfect dad, but I love my kids. I cherish one-on-one time with each of them. I try to make them feel special. Sometimes, I whisper: "You're my favorite, but don't tell the other kids." They know I tell each one the same thing, all except my youngest girl. When I tell her she's my favorite, she says I'm her favorite too. Gotta love that!

Everybody knows the story of Cinderella, how her prince had the shoe that fit her foot. Every little girl's dream is to be swept away by Prince Charming. In today's world, a girl will go to great lengths seeking a prince—some handsome guy who is fond of them. Not only do we long for real love and intimacy; we desire to be adored with eyes of love.

True Love's Kiss

It's in all the romance films, that moment when the guy and gal gaze at each other and kiss . . . or whatever. <Insert masculine eye roll here.> The key to these scenes, and their real-life parallel, is how the people look at one another. It's as if no one else on earth matters.

After being married for over twenty-two years, I have grown to like romance films. A recipe for a healthy marriage is to learn to love what your spouse loves.

One day, my wife had her girlfriends over, and my eldest son and I joined them in the living room to watch a love story. We were probably on our way to the fridge and something caught our eye. Well, we ended up watching more than we planned. (We weren't all that interested. I swear!)

In a climactic moment, the guy pursuing the girl gazed into her eyes and said something amazing. She melted in his arms. At that moment, I glanced at the women around me. They all had this tearful grin; I call it "the chick-flick face." We laugh about it to this day. To be honest, I may have teared up myself. I'm a bit of a crier. No shame, though! I cry in a manly way.

The reason people love stories like *Cinderella*, *The Princess Bride*, *Sleepless in Seattle* and *Die Hard* is because we were made to love and be loved. No shame in that. These films speak to our hearts. (Yippee Ki -Yay!)

In Search of True Love

Imagine for a moment a beautiful young girl growing up in a normal family. Despite her upbringing, she makes bad choices. She falls in love with the wrong people, gets rejected again and again, searches desperately for relief and ends up in a cycle of anguish, false hope, and despair. She realizes she's tragically unhappy. Something's missing, and she doesn't know what it is.

Unfortunately, this is a typical scenario for many people today. Looking for real love and finding none, they yearn to fill the void we have as humans—to be loved. Isn't that all we want? To be chosen, to be special, to be significant to someone else? Someone who whispers in our ear: "You're my favorite."

And to know it's true.

In today's house of mirrors masquerading as intimacy, we go from relationship to relationship, trying to fill our needs. We can't stop making wrong choices. We tell ourselves poor choices are better than no choices, but the fact is, we don't know how to make good choices. We don't know what true love is because we've never been truly loved. We don't know what it is to be chosen.

> A healing balm reaching the scar tissue of a damaged soul, awakening dead areas, calling them to life.

Indeed, there's not a human being who hasn't felt the pain of rejection, abandonment, and emptiness. It's real, and it feels like forever. Just another bleeding scar that'll never heal. *That's what scars do, right?*

Well . . . yes . . . and no. Your pain is real. So is God's healing.

Maybe there's a love you've never experienced, at least not at a level to heal your wounds. A love too good to be true. Yet it exists. Sounds scandalous, doesn't it? It is. But also know: it's not always easy.

Love incurs pain. It's the pain of believing . . . one more time . . . when all hope has been lost. It's the pain of opening an area you sealed off forever as an act of triage. It's a healing balm reaching the scar tissue of a damaged soul, awakening dead areas, calling them to life. It's the chronically misshapen, arising at love's command, uncurling from a fetal position of catatonic survival and shedding their grave clothes. It's walking upright into the light.

The first steps toward love are the hardest; they're also totally worth it.

Then they took away the stone from the place where the dead man was lying. And Jesus lifted up His eyes and said,

"Father, I thank You that You have heard Me. And I know that You always hear Me, but because of the people who are standing by I said this, that they may believe that You sent Me."

Now when He had said these things, He cried with a loud voice, "Lazarus, come forth!"

And he who had died came out bound hand and foot with graveclothes, and his face was wrapped with a cloth. Jesus said to them, "Loose him, and let him go."

JOHN 11:41-44 NKJV

Who Is This Woman?

Consider this scandalous story, one you may already know. I want you to approach it with fresh eyes and be open to new revelation. Allow yourself to experience the depths of Jesus' love and acceptance through this story. Let it be a wave of healing oil from the very heart of God.

In John chapter 4, we read of the woman at the well.

Now he had to go through Samaria. So he came to a town in Samaria called Sychar, near the plot of ground Jacob had given to his son Joseph.

Jacob's well was there, and Jesus, tired as he was from the journey, sat down by the well. It was about noon.

When a Samaritan woman came to draw water, Jesus said to her, "Will you give me a drink?" (His disciples had gone into the town to buy food.)

The Samaritan woman said to him, "You are a Jew and I

am a Samaritan woman. How can you ask me for a drink?"
(For Jews do not associate with Samaritans.)

Jesus answered her, "If you knew the gift of God and who it
is that asks you for a drink, you would have asked him and
he would have given you living water."

"Sir," the woman said, "you have nothing to draw with and
the well is deep. Where can you get this living water? Are
you greater than our father Jacob, who gave us the well and
drank from it himself, as did also his sons and his livestock?"

Jesus answered, "Everyone who drinks this water will be
thirsty again, but whoever drinks the water I give them will
never thirst. Indeed, the water I give them will become in
them a spring of water welling up to eternal life."

The woman said to him, "Sir, give me this water so that
I won't get thirsty and have to keep coming here to draw
water."

He told her, "Go, call your husband and come back."

"I have no husband," she replied.

Jesus said to her, "You are right when you say you have no
husband. The fact is, you have had five husbands, and the
man you now have is not your husband. What you have
just said is quite true."

Who was this woman? She was a Samaritan, someone who
was disdained for her ethnicity. There was such a chasm between
Jews and Samaritans that they didn't even eat together. In those
cultures, sharing a meal was an act of intimacy shared only with
someone your heart was open to.

Some think she was an adulterous woman. Jesus seemed to convict her when he told her she had been with five men, and that the one she was with now was not her husband. Yet the real story is about more than her relationship issues.

In digging deeper, I discovered a greater revelation of God's love in this story. As I looked closer at where Jesus revealed her life, my religious perspective unraveled. I was undone. Look at the story again.

"I have no husband," she replied.

Jesus said to her, "You are right when you say you have no husband. The fact is, you have had five husbands, and the man you now have is not your husband. What you have just said is quite true."

JOHN 4:17-18 NIV

Why do we assume she divorced all these other men and was now "living in sin" with her current boyfriend? The Scripture doesn't say this. In fact, a language study reveals something remarkable. When Jesus said, "You have had five husbands, and the man you now have is not your husband," in

> **Why do we assume she divorced all these other men and was now "living in sin" with her current boyfriend?**

the original language, this could mean: "You had five husbands but the one who proposed to you hasn't set a date yet."

Well, that changes things, doesn't it?

What about the other five husbands? We don't really know, but to help us understand some possibilities, we must examine marriage customs in her culture. Samaritans, like Jews, were under the law of Moses. Under the law, she couldn't have divorced her husbands; they would have divorced her. Further, if this woman was committing adultery, she could have faced major consequences, including a possible death sentence. We see this in John's gospel in the story of a woman caught in adultery (ref. John 8). Being killed was a real possibility.

First century culture was very oppressive towards women. They were often mistreated. This is why, when examining the life of Jesus, it was remarkable how he treated women. He supported them, loved them, and opened his heart to them. This was not culturally acceptable. Yet Mary Magdalene sat at the table with the other male disciples. This was revolutionary! One might even say: *scandalous!*

> **Was this a voice of conviction or compassion? Possibly both, but certainly not condemnation.**

It was common for a Jewish or Samaritan man to legally divorce his wife for trivial reasons. Making matters worse, once a woman was cast off by her husband, her prospects for survival were bleak. Which is why many ended up living lives involving adultery. Yet what if the woman at the well was not an adulterous woman living in sin? Certainly, it's possible she was committing adultery. Yet it's also possible that she was left and divorced by the five husbands! And the one she was engaged to had not set a wedding date. This happens today; some couples date for years without making a commitment. In some ways, culture hasn't changed. Both believers and unbelievers create loopholes to avoid true love's vows.

At the well, Jesus' intent might have been completely different. Consider this paraphrase: "Listen, I know it didn't work out with these other guys, and the one you are with now won't put a ring on it."

See? Was he exposing her sin or her wounds of rejection and abandonment? Was this a voice of conviction or compassion? Possibly both, but certainly not condemnation. Look at how she responded with a question about religion. She was intrigued. Had Jesus' words been taken as condemnation, her reaction would have been different, possibly involving language not suitable for this publication.

Clearly, she wasn't a mere sinner to Jesus. She was a thirsty woman at the well of living water . . . and she didn't know it yet.

All's Well That Ends Well

Historically, a well was more than a water source. It was a social gathering, a place women went to be noticed and chosen, providing a chance to find their Prince Charming. We see this throughout Scripture. Moses met his wife at a well. Abraham sent his servant to find his son a wife at a well. Jacob met his wife at a well. This scene in John's gospel provides the imagery of a groom choosing his bride, a parallel for a future pairing of Christ with his bride—the church.

Still, none of that was going through the woman's mind when she talked to this stranger who had the temerity to ask her for a drink. What was she searching for? And was Jesus also searching for her? She may have gone to this well far too many times. Yet it wasn't about the water; it was about the gaping hole in her heart, seeking someone who would love her. Looking for love. But this time she found eternal love. This time there was someone holding the proverbial slipper that fit her foot.

> Yet it wasn't about the water; it was about the gaping hole in her heart, seeking someone who would love her.

We call those moments *divine appointments*, or encounters with God's love. Even when we hide, he always seems to find us. After Adam and Eve turned away from communion with God, they hid (ref. Genesis 3). We also hide in our darkness, pain, and shame. But even when Adam and Eve ran, God pursued them. That's just who God is; he can't let us go! Jesus' encounter with the woman at the well resounds with the same heart we see in

Genesis 3: "Where are you?" Which could also mean: "Why are you hiding? I love you!" If you listen closely, you can hear a groom calling his bride.

The Place for the Thirsty

The Samaritan woman found herself at that same old well: "the place for the thirsty." We've all been there; maybe we are there right now.

Hoping to be noticed, she stands with her waterpot and empty heart, hiding her pain while trying to fill the void with something that could never satisfy. I imagine her propping herself at the edge of that old well, peering into the abyss, knowing there's water down there but unsure how to reach it. The desert sun pours down on her. Other women jostle for position, vying for attention, but she ignores them. Breaking her reverie, she hears a male voice cutting through the din. "Give me a drink." She may have heard that phrase before from others seeking to quench a different type of thirst.

> **Today was different. God set his own date for her. This day, she would meet her prince.**

This was different, however. There was life in these words, a distinct sound calling her to something new. Maybe she thought it was too good to be true. *A calling to real intimacy this time?* You see, it didn't matter what she had done, whether it was multiple divorces or even shacking up with someone. Jesus met her where she was, adulterous woman or not. She may have been engaged to another man. She may have been rejected five times by five husbands. None of this mattered to Jesus.

Today was different. God set his own date for her. This day, she would meet her prince. This would be the seventh man to share her life, yet this one was wooing her into a different kind of intimacy, one deep within her soul and spirit. It was a love under the gaze of the Father.

Wow! A much different take on the story. We are so quick to assume someone's past. We forget that Jesus came to set the captives free.

"Now he [Jesus] had to go through Samaria." Talk about a divine appointment! Maybe this moment, reading this book, is a divine appointment for you. I hope so. Heaven is open and he's pouring his love on your life. Receive it now and join your life to his.

Too Broken?

This revelation has led our church family to appreciate, love and accept many modern-day examples of the woman at the well. One in recent memory was Monique.

When Monique starting coming to our church, it was obvious that she carried a lot of history with her, and a lot of plastic surgery. Saying little to anyone, she always sat on the front row. I didn't know much about her but she always wanted a hug. She was broken. The first service she attended, we had a guest speaker. We met her and prayed with her. Over time, we learned her story. She continued to weep in the presence of the Lord, and the Father's love poured into her week after week.

> When we let the love of God arrest our hearts in a deep way, we see the world differently, and we will be able to bring the change it needs.

Her birth name was Michael. Starting at nine years old, she was raped and beaten by her father. As an adult, she fully transitioned to a transgender woman. We didn't judge her. We didn't have all the answers. All we knew how to do was love her. One day, she came to us for prayer specifically for her health. She was

HIV positive. My spirit rose within me. *Absolutely! I have to pray for this person.*

You see, when we walk in the Father's love, every encounter becomes a divine appointment. When we let the love of God arrest our hearts in a deep way, we see the world differently, and we will be able to bring the change it needs. We don't criticize the lack. We become the more.

We prayed wholeness and healing for Monique. God is the healer and we believe that. A couple weeks later, she told us her doctor said the HIV was nearly undetectable in her system. Wow! A supernatural miracle. Some may ask, "Did you fast and intercede?" No, we just loved! We have said for years, "Love people for who they are, right where they are, and they will become who they are supposed to be." We are not created to be the Holy Spirit to people. Simply love people, speak truth when they give you access to their heart, but do not be a religious Pharisee to them. We are created to see people through the eyes of the King. This is how we advance the kingdom of God. The Holy Spirt opens our eyes to see the kingdom, and it looks like broken souls needing love. It stirs our hearts. We are moved when we encounter people like Monique. We don't know everyone's history or why they did what they did, but we are called to love them, even if all they want is to weep and receive prayer and hugs. Lots of hugs.

My prayer, my cry, is that we would be like Jesus. He *had* to go through Samaria; there was no other choice. One encounter with Jesus can lead an entire city to Jesus.

From Well to Wellspring

Imagine a person like Monique or the Samaritan woman—someone searching for love and being rejected over and over again. I think we can all identify with these stories and how Jesus revealed his love and acceptance to them. Once we discover the source of true acceptance, we don't have to go back to the wells of temporal satisfaction.

*Jesus answered, "Everyone who drinks this water will be
thirsty again, but whoever drinks the water I give them will
never thirst. Indeed, the water I give them will become in
them a spring of water welling up to eternal life."*

JOHN 4:13-14 NIV

This living water becomes a wellspring on the inside, leading
to eternal life. The acceptance of the One heals the rejection of
many.

Jesus told this woman, "You don't have to look for false acceptance anymore." Yet sometimes we would rather be accepted for
a fake version of ourselves than risk being rejected for the real
version. Here is the good news: Come as you are; Jesus receives
you. You don't have to search for true love anymore. His true love
has pursued you and has found you. He is gazing at you right
now with fiery eyes of love. He is smiling over you, saying, "I have
what you've been looking for. I know you're thirsty. I have living
water that will truly quench your thirst."

No more searching for a lover's glance. His eyes of love are on
you. He's saying, "I choose you!"

God's love is so scandalous! Let him pour his tender affection
into your heart and soul right now. He is healing you! You are
totally accepted by him. You may have been rejected many times
over and felt like you were not the one, his favorite, but now you
can come under the gaze of the lover of all lovers.

Leave Your Waterpot

The ending of the woman's story is brilliant.

*The woman then left her waterpot, went her way into the
city, and said to the men, "Come, see a man who told me all
things that I ever did. Could this be the Christ?" Then they
went out of the city and came to him.*

JOHN 4:28-30 NKJV

Notice what the Samaritan woman did after her encounter with Jesus. "The woman then left her waterpot." She left the object that represented her past, her rejection, her shame, her mistakes. I encourage you to leave behind your waterpot and whatever that represents to your old life!

After abandoning her past, she shared her encounter with Jesus with those around her. It resulted in a revival.

> So there were many from the Samaritan village who became believers in Jesus because of the woman's testimony: "He told me everything I ever did!" Then they begged Jesus to stay with them, so he stayed there for two days, resulting in many more coming to faith in him because of his teachings. Then the Samaritans said to the woman, "We no longer believe just because of what you told us, but now we've heard him ourselves and are convinced that he really is the true Savior of the world!"
>
> JOHN 4:39-42

Because of her, many believed in Jesus and begged him to stay. There is a healing presence to Jesus, and they wanted it. It was scandalous for a Samaritan to believe the words of a Jewish rabbi, let alone declare: "He really is the true Savior of the world!"

She left the object that represented her past, her rejection, her shame, her mistakes.

Notice her testimony to her people: "He told me everything I ever did." This is remarkable considering the brevity of Jesus' conversation with her. He simply identified her search for love and himself as the answer. From: "You have had five husbands," to "I who speak to you am He."

That's it. And yet . . . that was everything she ever did. Her quest for love summed up her entire life.

Yes! The savior of all humanity. Every nation, tribe, and tongue, all radically loved by the Father, Son, and Holy Spirit.

The Focus of His Love

Let's read Ephesians 1:3-6 in *The Message* translation.

How blessed is God! And what a blessing he is! He's the Father of our Master, Jesus Christ, and takes us to the high places of blessing in him. Long before he laid down earth's foundations, he had us in mind, and had settled on us as the focus of his love, to be made whole and holy by his love. Long, long ago he decided to adopt us into his family through Jesus Christ. (What pleasure he took in planning this!) He wanted us to enter into the celebration of his lavish gift-giving by the hand of his beloved Son.

We are the focus of God's love. Isn't that beautiful? Before he created anything, he already thought about you and me and all of humanity. Let that sink in. The Godhead—Father, Son, and the Holy Spirit—chose to include us into this love. Talk about being chosen for something great! We're in the inner circle. Take a moment. Take a deep breath. And know that he is closer than the air you breathe. You are beloved. It's true. From now on: BE LOVED!

You no longer have to search for love in all the wrong places. Love searched you out. You don't have to hide anymore. You have left that old life of not feeling good enough, not feeling accepted. Leave that waterpot behind. Drink deeply from the well of living water. Jesus is the only thing that can truly satisfy us all.

From Samaritan to Saint

In the traditions of the Orthodox Church, there lives the memory of St. Photini, a woman honored for her visit by Jesus, a woman broken and desperate for love, a woman who encountered true love as only God can give. The woman at the well, she who was once the lowest of the low, is revered by the church as a holy martyr and equal to the Apostles.

There is greatness within you as well. Your past wounds, mistakes, and rejection should not dictate your future! Let an encounter with Jesus be your future!

God can truly make broken things beautiful. It doesn't matter how broken you think you are. Jesus is here to bring wholeness and healing to your heart. God is great enough to whisper into your ears, "You're my favorite."

Reflection, Discussion, and Prayer

1. Jesus' conversation with the Samaritan woman was one of compassion and conviction, not condemnation. Has Jesus ever revealed your heart, and instead of shame, you experienced compassion?

2. Have you ever accepted your struggles as, "That's just the way I am"? What is Jesus saying to you about some of the things you struggle with? Take a moment to listen.

3. How has the acceptance of the One, Jesus, healed the rejection of many in your life?

4. Imagine Jesus meeting you at the well. Ask God what waterpots you need to release—the things you constantly refill but which don't yield lasting satisfaction.

CHAPTER SIX

THE JEALOUS LOVER

Meanwhile, the moment we get tired in the waiting, God's Spirit is right alongside helping us along. If we don't know how or what to pray, it doesn't matter. He does our praying in and for us, making prayer out of our wordless sighs, our aching groans. He knows us far better than we know ourselves, knows our pregnant condition, and keeps us present before God. That's why we can be so sure that every detail in our lives of love for God is worked into something good.

ROMANS 8:26-28 MSG

SCRIPTURE TELLS THAT GOD surrounds us with love and protection. Well, what about when we make mistakes? Does his love still protect us? When we are weak, does he turn away his love, maybe to teach us a lesson? What happens when we fall? I mean, fall hard—flat on our faces, suck-a-rug kind of fall? It's one thing to know we are loved in good times, but when we make bad choices, even after we encounter God, what do we do then?

Early in my marriage, my wife, Rachelle, and I frequently got into arguments on the way to church. This made it tough to engage in fellowship, worship, and Bible study. I felt like a failure . . . as a husband and a Christian. We still loved each other, but that feeling of failure is tough to deal with, especially when we know better.

As of this writing, Rachelle and I have been married over twenty-two years. So, do we still fight in the car on the way to church? No! We're much more mature now. We drive separately. Ha!

The truth is, God doesn't just love us when we're on our best behavior. His love for us is not limited to times when we are winning, at least in the eyes of the world. Rachelle likes to quote Brennan Manning: "There is the you that people see, then there's the rest of you. Let God love the rest of you." It's easy for us to imagine God loving the Sunday morning version of us, but what about the rest of us? God loves us in the midst of turmoil, conflict, and battles. He even loves us when we make really dumb choices.

A Custody Battle

One night towards the end of a powerful worship service, I was struck by a wild thought. I knew it was God speaking to my heart. *There is someone here who is going through a great custody battle, and I am going to give them favor and breakthrough!*

> "There is the you that people see, then there's the rest of you. Let God love the rest of you."

Well, me being me, I grabbed the microphone to share what God spoke to me. A young man in the congregation started weeping. He was easy to spot in the crowd. Covered in tattoos, he looked like the lead singer of a heavy metal band. I walked over and put my hand on his shoulder and continued to pray. I felt he was under a dark cloud of depression, hopeless and forlorn. As I continued to pray, he wept harder. God was moving powerfully in his life.

After the service, overwhelmed by God's touch, he told me about his custody battle; he had not seen his daughter in a year. I encouraged him to not to lose heart, but to believe God.

A few days later, the miraculous happened. The mother of his daughter emailed him and said she didn't want to fight in court anymore. She wanted him to see his daughter. That same week, he got to hug his little girl for the first time in over a year. Talk about God working in the midst of a battle!

This and countless other examples have taught me that God stays faithful, even in our struggles. Indeed, he actually brings greater breakthroughs to us in those times. This doesn't mean he is the cause of our conflicts and struggles, but he does work through those times for our good!

There is something to learn from these moments of conflict, and if we accept the lessons, we become more like the people God says we already are. Contradictory? Not if we understand who God is and how he operates. He calls into being things that were not.

As it is written: "I have made you a father of many nations."
He is our father in the sight of God, in whom he believed—
the God who gives life to the dead and calls into being
things that were not.

ROMANS 4:17 NIV

We learn who God is when we fail—those times when we forget who we really are. In failure, if we drift or fall away from him, he pursues us with a fiery love.

God's love is fierce. As the Apostle James wrote:

And do you suppose that God doesn't care? The proverb has
it that "he's a fiercely jealous lover." And what he gives in
love is far better than anything else you'll find.

JAMES 4:5 MSG

You don't often hear God called a "fiercely jealous lover." As humans, we tend to look at jealousy in a negative light. We associate it with stalking, domestic violence, and worse. Yet God's jealousy isn't like that. It isn't dark or paranoid but intense and powerful. It shows itself in conflict. God's jealous love burns for us when we face opposition. Indeed, what we call God's wrath is actually an extension of his love, because God *is* love. Wrath is God's "No!" hurled against our enemies even as he wraps us in love. It's his opposition to sin, not to his sons and daughters. God doesn't get upset like we do. Of course, we are created in his image, so our fierceness might resemble God's fierce love. But we are also works in progress, becoming the people God says we are, hence our less-than-perfect actions. Here's a story of one of those times I got a little too fierce.

A Fierce Encounter

I like to think of myself as a fierce lover. As a young man, I wanted to sweep Rachelle off of her feet, win her heart, make her my wife. At times, I acted tough to impress her. Now, it's normal for young men to bow up and get into conflicts when women are around. They want a tough guy, right? Well, sometimes they do. The trouble starts when we run into other tough guys trying to impress their women.

Years ago, I was on a street corner being harassed by three guys looking for trouble. *Well, they picked the wrong guy!* At least, that's what I thought as I rushed to the challenge.

The whole thing happened so fast. Thirty minutes prior, I was having dinner with Rachelle and the kids. It was a great night until we left the restaurant. We were in separate cars and she left before me. Suddenly, there was a word here, a shove there, and punches flew, fists landed and bodies hit the ground. I ended up tripping backwards over one of my attackers and smacked my head against the pavement. As I lay partially conscious, they positioned me for a curb check—placing my face against the curb to stomp my head. They could have killed me.

As these crazed punks prepared to crush my skull, I heard Rachelle's voice, the love of my life, scream: "STOP! He's a father!" I didn't even know she was there. She saw the fight and turned around.

I'll never forget that moment. She saved my life.

What a strange thing to yell into a violent encounter: *He's a father!* But it worked. The three guys about to kick my face into darkness scattered like kitchen roaches in light. And no wonder. Rachelle's voice was fierce, declarative, a war cry protecting the father of her children and the husband she dearly loved. It was the love of God resident in this lovely woman, ready to charge hell for her man. Indeed, she did.

As I prepared this manuscript, God reminded me of the incident. *The way Rachelle spoke over you is the same way I do, even in the midst of great conflict.* He had my attention now. *I will speak straight to your identity and tell you who you are, even when you fall flat on your face, because I love you with a jealous love!*

It reminds me of the song by Elyssa Smith from Upperroom Worship: "Surrounded."

> *It may look like I'm surrounded*
> *But I'm surrounded by You*
> *This is how I fight my battles*

Wow! So even in the midst of our bad choices, flat on our backs, encircled by enemies, we are surrounded by our loving God. The help from heaven is here! He lives within us. The Spirit of truth is a fierce, jealous lover. He declares who we really are. He shouts to our innermost being that we are beloved children of God. We are his kids! He tells us that we are not our current actions nor situation. We are who he says we are, called into being by his creative voice. *He's my child!*

> *I will speak straight to your identity and tell you who you are, even when you fall flat on your face, because I love you with a jealous love!*

I'll bet you could recall moments like this with the Lord. Ask the Holy Spirit to show you how he might have spoken to you in the midst of conflict. And then agree with who he says you are.

He Has the Final Say

Here's an idea. If God himself calls us *his kids*, and if God calls us *saints*, not just *sinners saved by grace*, then maybe we should take him at his word. Who could possibly know more about our true identity than God himself? He created us and has the ultimate say in who we are.

God speaks to us by his Holy Spirit, both in good times and bad. It's exactly what a loving parent would do . . . or a fierce wife. (Incidentally, she was not too happy with me after that fight. *Next time, walk away, fool!*)

In the midst of conflict, just like Rachelle's "He's a father!" the Holy Spirit speaks straight to our identity. You could be getting beat up by life, and the Spirit of God will declare exactly who you are. Indeed, our identity is our protection, our strength. God loves us so much; he cannot stand for us to be unaware of who we are. We are his.

I have two sons and three daughters. I'd be heartbroken if they forgot their identity and the value it conveys. My kids are more valuable than anything in the world. God feels the exact same way.

Words are powerful, so powerful that God literally spoke the universe into existence. The Bible says:

> In the same way, the Spirit helps us in our weakness. We do not know what we ought to pray for, but the Spirit himself intercedes for us through wordless groans.
> ROMANS 8:26 NIV

And when our words fail, we can rely on the Word of God. His love speaks to us, through us, and for us. Just as Rachelle spoke to my identity as a father when I was a fool, God speaks to our true identity even when we are hell-bent on proving him wrong. We need to believe what God says about us; it's our new reality in Christ Jesus.

This is why, as sons and daughters of God, we feel convicted when we go against our new identity. Yet this isn't about guilt and shame; there is enough of that from our old religious mindset. Let's lose that terrible way of thinking. Romans 8:1 (NIV) tells us: "There is now no condemnation for those who are in Christ Jesus."

So, what is the difference between a godly conviction and ungodly condemnation? It's in knowing our true identity. Condemnation tells us we are criminals, worthy of punishment. Holy conviction tells us we are children of God, worthy of so much more than our mistakes allow us to believe. Reject the voice of mistakes! Believe the voice of God! He loves us, and he really wants the best for us.

> **Condemnation tells us we are criminals, worthy of punishment. Holy conviction tells us we are children of God, worthy of so much more than our mistakes allow us to believe.**

The reason we feel vexed when we sin or fall is because the Holy Spirit is letting us know that our true identity is pure. And what is that identity? That we have been joined to Christ and made new in him. We are royalty!

> *My old identity has been co-crucified with Christ and no longer lives. And now the essence of this new life is no longer mine, for the Anointed One lives his life through me—we live in union as one! My new life is empowered by the faith of the Son of God who loves me so much that he gave himself for me, dispensing his life into mine!*
>
> GALATIANS 2:20 TPT

Mortal Combat

Of course, all this is just talk until put to the test.

I had just returned home for the day when I received a call saying Rachelle's fifteen-year-old sister, Naomi, was gone, the victim of a medication mix that stopped her heart and breathing. She had no pulse for over forty-five minutes. The paramedics had already tried to resuscitate her. Now they were fighting to get my mother-in-law away from Naomi's corpse. She refused and continued to fiercely pray.

As soon as I heard these words, faith came over me as an emphatic "NO!" I prayed strongly for thirty seconds, then got on the phone with Rachelle and told my mother-in-law to put me on speaker. Although we were not in the same room, nor even the same state, we knew that something miraculous was about to happen. I loudly declared: "I command life and breath to fill Naomi right now, in the name of Jesus!"

In that moment, Naomi took a deep breath and sat up! In the midst of this conflict with death itself, God gave Naomi newness of life, the power of Jesus' resurrection! She is alive today and married with six beautiful children.

It's in the midst of mortal combat that we encounter the truth of life and death. It's hard to read these words as anything but the very life of God:

> *The Spirit of God, who raised Jesus from the dead, lives in you. And just as God raised Christ Jesus from the dead, he will give life to your mortal bodies by this same Spirit living within you.*
>
> ROMANS 8:11 NLT

As we awaken to the reality that God has joined us to himself and completely transformed our identity, we will walk in newness of life! We can read the Bible through many different lenses, some of which are scratched and warped. I've discovered that the clearest lens is the person of Jesus himself. If we don't read the Bible through the life of Christ, we get a distorted picture.

For example, Paul tells us, "For those who are led by the Spirit of God are the children of God" (Rom. 8:14 NIV). Simple enough, yet it can be easily misread: "For those *who want to be* children of God should be led by the Spirit of God."

See the difference? In reality, Scripture tells us the truth of our identity. We *are* the children of God; therefore, we *are* led by the Holy Spirit. Identity always comes before action. A bird doesn't fly to *become* a bird. A bird flies *because* it's a bird.

When God introduced himself to Moses one bush-burning, desert day, he didn't identify himself as who he wanted to be. No, he declared who he was . . . now and forevermore: "I AM!" (ref. Exodus 3:14). My friends, as the redeemed in Christ, now and forevermore: you *are!*

> **Identity always comes before action. A bird doesn't fly to become a bird. A bird flies because it's a bird.**

In Genesis 1, the first creatures God blessed were the birds of the air and the fish in the sea. God essentially said: "Let the fish swim throughout the vastness of the sea, and let the birds fly through the heavens." This is a fingerprint of God. He loves to create free things to swim and soar. Like birds, we are created to soar in our identity. That doesn't mean absolute freedom to do whatever we want. Rather, it means the freedom to do whatever we were created to do in God. He is the one who shapes our true identity.

Understanding how identity precedes behavior is essential to experience transformation. Who you are is not determined by what you do. As a child of God, all that rotten, nasty stuff from your past does not define you. The fact that you are an adopted son or daughter of the creator of heaven and earth means that even your worst behavior doesn't own you. Only God defines you, and he wants you to have freedom. Let that sink in. The only one who has any right to control you, doesn't want to control you! You are free to be who God created you to be!

Even though God has given us freedom, there are still many factors to every choice we make. Bad choices come from bad information—about ourselves and the world around us. Our actions are, to a large extent, determined by how we see ourselves. If you see yourself as successful, your actions will align with success. Likewise, if you identify as a failure, you'll align with failure. This doesn't mean that we aren't free. Quite the contrary. It means we are free to make decisions based on how we see ourselves. With this freedom comes responsibility.

Through a Glass Darkly

Now we see things imperfectly, like puzzling reflections in a mirror, but then we will see everything with perfect clarity. All that I know now is partial and incomplete, but then I will know everything completely, just as God now knows me completely.

1 CORINTHIANS 13:12 NLT

Unfortunately, we often see ourselves with a cracked and cloudy mirror, broken by our past and obscured by condemnation. Every wrong thing done to us, every abuse, every broken promise, all the bad we've done and even the good, can give us a distorted view of who we are. When we see ourselves through a marred reflection, it distorts who God says we are. Yet Paul says: "God now knows me completely." Let's look into the mirror of love and believe God!

The direction of our gaze is equally important. Emphasizing our past allows it to control us. I don't want to minimize genuine trauma; certainly, there are deep issues that should be dealt with. People need healing. But we must walk through it and move on. Letting past abuse dictate our future only honors our abuser. Identifying with our problems and bad habits causes us to repeat them. It's time to let go of the past and enjoy the love of God that is very real in this present moment.

When I made the choice to fight those guys, I was seeing myself in a fractured mirror, distorted by sin and my own failure.

It only led to more sin and failure, and could have killed me! "The wages of sin is death" (Rom. 6:23). I'm living proof that you are not the bad things that you've done. Remember, the cross does not *confer* your value. The cross *confirms* your value to God. The Father sees a son or daughter, a flawless reflection of Jesus Christ. He seeks you out in the midst of your conflict and brokenness and declares you fully his.

The best part is that the Lord doesn't heal our fractured mirror; he removes it. He'll do that right now if you ask. "Lord, how do you see me?" You are his child. His love is furious. He longs to show us who we really are.

The Apostle John understood this. He described himself as the disciple whom Jesus loved. What an amazing revelation to have! To realize that God loves us as his only child. John knew his identity. He knew the passion God had for him. He knew his identity better than anybody. How revolutionary would it be if we could look in the mirror and see the one whom Jesus loved. Here's a secret. (Don't tell the others.) Jesus didn't love John any more than he loves you . . . right now . . . right here. God loves you as much as any Bible hero. You are the one who Jesus loves.

> **How revolutionary would it be if we could look in the mirror and see the one whom Jesus loved.**

Flawless in His Eyes

My dad is a successful entrepreneur. Years ago, he owned a mortgage company, and he hired me for a commission-only position. It was a new venture for me, outside my comfort zone, but I trusted my dad as my mentor. He has a special gift for business. At the time, I was newly married, with a newborn baby, struggling financially and mired in debt. I was tired of bank overdraft fees and the stress that they brought.

So I took the leap, worked long hours my first month, and it paid off! I got my first commission check, and it was nearly double what I made at my previous job! Dad walked me to the bank to cash the check. As the teller counted out the one-hundred-dollar bills, I had a silly grin on my face. I couldn't wait to tell Rachelle that we had more than enough to get caught up and that our bank account would no longer be overdrawn. As the bank teller placed the last bill on the fat stack of Benjamins, Dad looked at me with fierce admiration and said, "Now remember how easy it was to make this money. You have it in your DNA, Son!"

This was a game-changer! I had entrepreneur genes just like he did!

As good as it is to make an honest dollar, here's better news. Our heavenly Dad owns the bank of righteousness, and he has kindly allowed us to participate in his business. He has made a fat deposit of forgiveness in our overdrawn sin accounts and has fully accredited us with his righteousness. Not only that, but our Father-God has infused our DNA with the ability—by grace—to produce righteousness!

> "Now remember how easy it was to make this money. You have it in your DNA, Son!"

I will never forget what Dad did for me that day. He changed my mindset from poverty to abundance. I have been walking in blessing ever since.

God reminded me of this moment when I was reading the book of Romans:

> *Our faith in Jesus transfers God's righteousness to us, and he now declares us flawless in his eyes. This means we can now enjoy true and lasting peace with God, all because of what our Lord Jesus, the Anointed One, has done for us. Our faith guarantees us permanent access into this marvel-*

ous kindness that has given us a perfect relationship with
God. What incredible joy bursts forth within us as we keep
on celebrating our hope of experiencing God's glory!

ROMANS 5:1-2 TPT

Let these words speak into your life. You are flawless in his eyes! Your relationship with God may not yet be perfected, but his relationship with you is perfect! It's vital to know we are righteous before him and that righteous living can flow from our lives. From this point on, see your spiritual account as accredited with the righteousness of Christ. You are a righteous entrepreneur. Your DNA produces righteous living.

Lord Have Mercy

I want to conclude this chapter with a revelation that changed my life. It's about grace. Like many who read the Bible, I thought grace and mercy were the same thing. I was wrong.

Mercy is encompassed within the broader scope of grace. Thus, they are similar but not identical. Mercy is what we should be thankful for if we forget who we are and fall. Mercy is the cushion that catches us in our rapid descent.

Grace, on the other hand, isn't mercy. It's actually God's nature, love and power that flows from heaven to us. Grace empowers us to get back up and walk. The ancient church called God's grace "divine energy." Imagine that!

Consider the man at the pool of Bethesda (ref. John 5). The Bible says it had five porches—five is the number of grace—therefore Bethesda means "House of Grace." There is a message here! The man was lame for thirty-eight years, during which he lay on a mat. His infirmity dictated his entire life: where he went, what he did, his history, and future. He needed someone to put him into the water at the right time to receive his healing.

So, when Jesus asked him: "Do you want to be made well?" the sick man answered: "Sir, I have no man to put me into the pool when the water is stirred up; but while I am coming, another steps down before me" (John 5:6-7 NKJV).

Notice that the man didn't really answer Jesus' question. Instead, he lamented his lot in life. We do the same thing. Jesus asks if we want freedom, and we offer excuses to justify why we are not free. *Well, Lord. You see, there's this mat.*

> **Jesus revealed grace. This same grace raises us to take dominion over the things that once oppressed us.**

Jesus responded to the man in grace—not just graciously, but in the power of grace.

Jesus said to him, "Rise, take up your bed and walk." And immediately the man was made well, took up his bed, and walked.

JOHN 5:8-9 NKJV

At the Pool of Bethesda, amidst the brokenness and suffering, Jesus revealed grace. This same grace raises us to take dominion over the things that once oppressed us. Grace is a person; his name is Jesus! Grace is God's power for reigning in life.

Look at what Paul says about God's grace in Romans:

For if by the one man's offense death reigned through the one, much more those who receive abundance of grace and of the gift of righteousness will reign in life through the One, Jesus Christ.

ROMANS 5:17 NKJV

Not only is God's love scandalous, especially in conflict, but his grace empowers us to rise and overcome. Grace is God's divine supernatural enablement to walk in our new identity. It's divine energy when we are weary!

Receive grace and rise in your godly identity to reign in life!

Reflection, Discussion, and Prayer

1. How does the proper understanding of grace affect your faith, emotions, and confidence?

2. Think of a time in your life when you were in the midst of a battle and God spoke directly to the core of your identity.

3. Reflect on how you can practically see yourself in the mirror that the Holy Spirit gives you.

4. Consider the mats in life that you lie on, unable to move, waiting for a deliverer. Is it possible that Jesus is calling you to pick up your mat, rise in his grace (divine energy), and walk in your new identity?

CHAPTER SEVEN

IT'S GOD'S FAULT!

We are pressed on every side by troubles, but we are not crushed. We are perplexed, but not driven to despair. We are hunted down, but never abandoned by God. We get knocked down, but we are not destroyed. Through suffering, our bodies continue to share in the death of Jesus so that the life of Jesus may also be seen in our bodies.

2 CORINTHIANS 4:8-10 NLT

WHEN GOD CREATED HUMAN beings in his own image, he gave us a free will—the freedom to choose. And while free will has its appeal, with that freedom comes the risk of hurting ourselves and creation itself. Human beings are powerful creatures with the ability to say yes or no to everything, including God. Further, a free will means God is not in exhaustive control of our lives. This is because free will and control are mutually exclusive. God can't both control us and give us the ability—indeed, the responsibility—to make our own choices.

This is important because without free will, there would be no opportunity for love. Real love requires relationship, and relationship requires choice. That's just the way it is. So, when God created us in his image, he allowed for the possibility of humanity choosing to turn away from him. He relinquished control of humanity in a bid for a loving relationship with us.

Despite these facts, it's common to hear someone say, "Well, God allowed <this or that> to happen." The context is usually something bad. Yet it's not that simple. It would be more accurate to say that God allowed the possibility of suffering or evil when he created the world. If we think it's merely God allowing certain things and not allowing other things, we are viewing God through a lens that distorts God's true nature and the system he created. The view of God as one who exhaustively and meticulously controls our lives is a god made in our image. Control is what we humans tend to do, and some do it more than others. The drive to control our environment is rooted in fear and insecurity. God, however, is not insecure nor afraid. God doesn't control things; it's not in his nature. However, God is the source of life itself, and he sustains life by his love and grace.

> *If it were his [God's] intention*
> *and he withdrew his spirit and breath,*
> *all humanity would perish together*
> *and mankind would return to the dust.*
> JOB 34:14-15 NIV

Life, by its nature, involves freedom to choose. For mankind, the most important choice we make is to remain in God's love, communing with him and not turn away from him. This was the same choice Adam and Eve faced, with disastrous consequences.

> *Then the man and his wife heard the sound of the Lord God*
> *as he was walking in the garden in the cool of the day, and*
> *they hid from the Lord God among the trees of the garden.*
> *But the Lord God called to the man, "Where are you?"*
> GENESIS 3:8-9 NIV

As a Father

I love my five children and they love me. They are made partially in my image. (Fortunately, they get their looks from their mom.) So, as they receive my love, it's natural for them to love me back. Relationship involves love reciprocated.

I'm not a perfect dad, but I love my kids as any good father should, and I hope they stay in relationship with me. They know I want the best for them. I am their father and would do anything to see them succeed. I support their passions, creativity, and dreams. But because they are free to love or not to love, they may make choices that could harm our relationship and ultimately harm themselves. It wouldn't be healthy for any of my kids to turn away from me and my love, but they have that choice. They could go forth and live without a relationship with me, but I hope they don't.

Yet with God, we are utterly dependent upon his divine love and communion in order to live. Sure, we can live as if he doesn't exist. We can ignore his presence in our lives and disregard the evidence that he fills all of creation. But eventually, we will run out of life and cease to be. Apart from the vine, the fruit dies . . . slowly.

That's what happened in the garden. Under the influence of the serpent, Adam and Eve questioned who God was and what he said, and that led them to question their own identity. This steadily increased the distance between themselves and their Creator. The decisions that followed this gradual separation opened the door to sin, inflicting death upon all humanity.

Therefore, just as sin entered the world through one man, and death through sin, and in this way death came to all people, because all sinned.

ROMANS 5:12 NIV

The fact is, we were not designed to live apart from God. When God made us in his image, he also delegated authority to humanity to reign in this world and care for creation.

God blessed them and said to them, "Be fruitful and increase in number; fill the earth and subdue it. Rule over

*the fish in the sea and the birds in the sky and over every
living creature that moves on the ground."*

GENESIS 1:26 NIV

The Amplified Bible is a bit clearer here:

*Then God said, "Let Us (Father, Son, Holy Spirit) make man
in Our image, according to Our likeness [not physical, but
a spiritual personality and moral likeness]; and let them
have complete authority over the fish of the sea, the birds
of the air, the cattle, and over the entire earth, and over
everything that creeps and crawls on the earth."*

Consider the phrase: "complete authority." That's a powerful
assignment. Yet our God-given authority was never intended to
be separated from partnership with God. To do so is to "sow the
wind and reap the whirlwind" (Hos. 8:7 NIV).

True Sovereignty

All of this discussion brings us to the concept of God's sovereignty—the idea that God can do whatever he wants, whenever
he wants. Does God as sovereign mean he exercises complete
control of everything on earth? No. It means that God can still
be Lord of all and yet not control all. If he is truly sovereign, then
he can decide to be a super-controlling God or not.

But our God is in heaven; He does whatever He pleases.

PSALM 115:3 NKJV

If we don't think God can do what he pleases, we don't believe
he is sovereign. Besides, it takes more of a sovereign God to rule
with free-willed humans versus one that exhaustively micro-
manages his creation. Furthermore, Jesus has revealed God as a
Father presiding over creation, not that other guy in the sky.

As a Father, he guides, loves and is present to give us strength and power to live as he intends us to live—in communion with him, yielded to his heartbeat, carrying out his mandates. Note that he gave Adam and Eve their responsibilities in broad mandates, but he did not tell them precisely how to accomplish these. God is not a micro-manager.

To be accurate, our understanding of God's sovereignty must fit the image of God revealed in Jesus. I call this "the Jesus test." This father-son relationship is the foundation of this understanding. Jesus and his Father were one. His divine nature was eternally one with the Father, but his humanity yielded to him and operated in harmony with the Father. Jesus carried out the will, intent and desire of his Father. "He went about doing good and healing all who were oppressed by the devil, for God was with Him" (Acts 10:38 NASB). He revealed the heart, desire and intent of God the Father. Of course, the will and desire of God does not always happen. This is clearly seen in the prayer Jesus taught his disciples:

> **It takes more of a sovereign God to rule with free-willed humans versus one that exhaustively micromanages his creation.**

This, then, is how you should pray:
"Our Father in heaven,
hallowed be your name,
your kingdom come,
your will be done,
on earth as it is in heaven."
MATTHEW 6:9 NIV

Jesus taught us to pray that the Father's will would be done. Obviously, God has an intent for humanity that is not fully manifested. Still, we have his promise.

The Lord is not slack concerning His promise, as some count slackness, but is longsuffering toward us, not willing that any should perish but that all should come to repentance.
2 PETER 3:9 NKJV

God's intent is that people don't perish but instead are redeemed through Christ. Yet that doesn't always happen. People are given a choice to have relationship with God. We see in Scripture and in life that people actually reject him and perish (ref. Matthew 7:13-14, Revelation 21:8).

Powerless Victims

Now, none of this negates our obligation to live circumspect lives. Indeed, a free will, empowered by the Father's grace, requires and enables us to live responsibly. Not only are we to pray for the Father's will, but we are to partner with him to accomplish it! Just as Jesus did!

> **A wrong view of God's sovereignty leads people to live as powerless victims. According to God, we are neither.**

For God is working in you, giving you the desire and the power to do what pleases him.
PHILIPPIANS 2:13 NLT

Note the dual nature of God's grace: the desire and power to do well according to God. To quote the great prophet Ben Parker: "With great power comes great responsibility." (I read that on the web.)

A wrong view of God's sovereignty leads people to live as powerless victims. According to God, we are neither. We are called to both pray and partner with God to do his will because it's not being fully done. This partnership with God is something he chose. The apostle Paul reminds God's people of this truth.

For we are co-workers in God's service; you are God's field, God's building.

1 CORINTHIANS 3:8-9 NIV

The word *co-workers* is where we get the word *synergy*. Paul is talking about how we work together in partnership with heaven to invade earth. We have a role to play in this. We plant seeds, water and cultivate them, but God makes them grow. He has sovereignly chosen us to partner with him. There is no reason to live or think of ourselves as powerless victims. Let us rise up and walk in the authority that God gave us as sons and daughters, as we yield to him in perfect harmony . . . just as Jesus did!

> **God rules by relational love, not control.**

Iconic Omni-Being

Our view of God affects how we see the world and live our lives. The Bible reveals God as always being close to us. He is revealed as a caring Father who loves being near to his kids. He is not some iconic omni-being.

God rules by relational love, not control. He is love, as we read in 1 John. So, when we assume that God rules by micro-control, we are not seeing God as he is. Rather, we are seeing our version of God made in our own image. We are projecting how we would rule if we were God, because in our limited imaginations, we can't imagine any other way. Good thing we're not God.

There is a vast difference between Jesus as Lord and an exhaustively controlling deity. Yes, Jesus is Lord of all, but he is not in control of all, nor does he seek to be. Further, there is a healthy way to be utterly yielded and dependent upon Jesus, just as he was with his Father. We surrender our lives to him but we rise from this foundation and exercise our free wills. We judge matters, exercise wisdom, apply experience, make decisions, take action, and learn from our results. It's called life, and we live it to the fullest yielded to Jesus. Yes, Jesus surrendered in the garden, crying, "Not my will, but yours be done." Please understand, however, that Jesus did not remain in the garden. He surrendered, he rose up, and he did what he knew he had to do.

Although God could control everything, he chooses not to. We, on the other hand, are not equipped to control our world so we need to quit trying. Some of us can barely get dressed and out of the house each morning. We cannot control life, and we don't know everything. Peace comes as we disengage that desire to figure everything out. We are enveloped by a loving Father. We can rest in his love. He's got me; he's got you. God has sovereignly chosen to allow us the freedom to live life; he has graciously given us freedom to learn and grow.

It's the difference between swimming in the Pacific Ocean or hoarding every cup of it. The waves and tides, the surfers and whales, are all beyond our grasp. Our choice is to sink or swim; and we'll have more fun swimming.

Stuff Happens

Of course, bad things happen in life. We live in an imperfect world. People sin, commit acts of violence and harm natural things (like other people). Further, we all make imperfect choices, even bad choices, and natural laws exist beyond our control. Ever try arguing with gravity from the top of the Empire State building? I don't recommend it. Gravity wins every time. It came with creation, just like our freedom. Of course, it's not the fall you have to worry about. It's the sudden stop at the end.

Where is God when bad things happen? He's with us always, right? So where is he when bad stuff is going down? Here is a common verse people use to understand tragedy.

And we know that all things work together for good to those who love God, to those who are called according to His purpose.

ROMANS 8:28 NKJV

Now, this is Scripture, so we know it's true. What's not always true is our interpretation of Scripture. No matter what is written, we can still get it wrong through a distorted lens. Here, for example, we could read Romans 8:28 as:

And we know that God has divinely initiated all things for our good, to those who love Him, to those who are called according to His purpose.

BVV (BLURRY VISION VERSION)

Yes, *all things work together for good,* but that does not mean *God divinely initiates all things for our good.* Yet that's what we read because of our blurry spiritual vision. (It's common for us with many parts of the Bible.) There is a big difference between God initiating something to happen, and his amazing ability to take what happens in this broken world and turn it around for good. He is adept at making broken things beautiful; just look in the mirror! (#MadeInGodsImage.) God can truly take things that

> Yes, *all things work together for good,* but that does not mean *God divinely initiates all things for our good.*

harmed us and extract a fragrance of love from them. This is what this verse is saying. It's not some catch-all phrase for divine sovereignty. It means that God can take what is inferior or evil and change it into something good. He does that well; look at the cross. He is the Father of Lights, and every good and perfect gift comes from him! The fact is, God is not in control of our lives the way we may think; therefore he is not the cause of our troubles. However, he remakes all things for our benefit. Indeed, our greatest lessons come from our misfortunes. Welcome to Life-101. There will be a final exam at the end.

> *Don't be deceived, my dear brothers and sisters. Every good and perfect gift is from above, coming down from the Father of the heavenly lights, who does not change like shifting shadows.*
>
> JAMES 1:16-17 NKJV

A Reason for Everything?

In times of suffering, we often search for the reason something happened—the divine "why?" behind an event. Yet everything that happens doesn't need a reason. Thank God! We see in Romans 8 that a bad happening can be transformed into something beautiful, something aligned with God's heart for us. If God intended for us to suffer eternally under the reign of sin and death, he would never have become human to redeem and heal us from this world of brokenness.

> **Truth is far better than wrongly blaming God for some awful tragedy.**

In our search for the mysterious "why?" behind things, we come upon a slew of factors: natural laws, sin in the world, people's choices, spiritual forces, generational curses, butterflies in Singapore—take your pick! And yet some things have no why at all. They just are.

This is reality; it's the reality we live in, the reality God created for us. Truth is far better than wrongly blaming God for some awful tragedy. Truth is freeing.

> *Then you will know the truth, and the truth will set you free.*
>
> JOHN 8:32 NIV

Instead of asking God *why?* ask him *how?* Hey God:

- How are you going to shed your love and light amidst the brokenness and suffering?
- How are you going to take what the enemy meant for a curse and turn it into a blessing?
- How are your love and glory going to manifest in this devastation of death and destruction?

And with every question, apply your faith so that these challenges do not morph into doubt and unbelief. God *can* and *will* work a tragedy into a beautiful tapestry. Let's get rid of this idea that there is a divine "why?" behind everything. This understanding of God comes from Greek philosophy; it doesn't come from the revelation of God in the Bible, nor does it fit the perfect image of God we see in his Son Jesus.

The Son is the image of the invisible God, the firstborn over all creation.

COLOSSIANS 1:15 NIV

The Son is the radiance of God's glory and the exact representation of his being, sustaining all things by his powerful word. After he had provided purification for sins, he sat down at the right hand of the Majesty in heaven.

HEBREWS 1:3 NIV

Here's a powerful quote from a Christian theologian named David Bentley Hart, in his book *Doors of the Seas*.

A child dying an agonizing death from diphtheria, of a young mother ravaged by cancer, of tens of thousands of Asians swallowed in an instant by the sea, of millions murdered in death camps and gulags and forced famines....

Our faith is in a God who has come to rescue his creation from the absurdity of sin and the emptiness of death, and so we are permitted to hate these things with a perfect hatred. …As for comfort, when we seek it, I can imagine none greater than the happy knowledge that when I see the death of a child, I do not see the face of God, but the face of his enemy.

Incredible! I have been through some rough times in life. My blurry vision led me to believe it was God's fault, when it was really a combination of factors: my faults, circumstances beyond my control, other peoples' choices, natural laws of attraction, and the tidal forces of the moon. Still, it's easier to blame someone else for our mistakes. We tend to blame others around us, and we wrongly blame God, when we should own our choices. Yes, other things were in play, but I was the one who stepped into the arena. As long as we are blaming others, we are avoiding accountability leading to learning from our mistakes.

> **"I do not see the face of God, but the face of his enemy."**

We can attribute our tendency to avoid blame to man's fallen thinking. After they sinned, Adam and Eve hid from God, blamed each other (and the snake) for their predicament. Eventually, sinful humanity blamed God for everything in life.

He [God] said, "Who told you that you were naked? Have you eaten of the tree of which I commanded you not to eat?"

The man said, "The woman whom you gave to be with me, she gave me fruit of the tree, and I ate."

Then the Lord God said to the woman, "What is this that you have done?"

The woman said, "The serpent deceived me, and I ate."
GENESIS 3:11-13 ESV

In the book of Job, we read Job's journey from blaming God to repenting of his bad theology.

> *I know that you can do all things;*
> *no purpose of yours can be thwarted.*
> *You asked, "Who is this that obscures my plans without*
> *knowledge?"*
> *Surely I spoke of things I did not understand,*
> *things too wonderful for me to know.*
> *You said, "Listen now, and I will speak;*
> *I will question you,*
> *and you shall answer me."*
> *My ears had heard of you*
> *but now my eyes have seen you.*
> *Therefore I despise myself*
> *and repent in dust and ashes.*
> JOB 42:2-6 NIV

Job got it wrong, just as we do! Truth twisted is error most deceiving.

Closer Than We Can Comprehend

We were not designed to know everything, so turn off that internal switch that strives to be omniscient. Still, we want answers to our questions. Some can be answered; others cannot be answered. How can God be near the brokenhearted, near suffering, death or heartache? There are many things we don't fully understand, but when we look at the revelation of God through the singular event that impacted the cosmos like none other, we can gaze at a beautiful mystery. This event is the incarnation of God in the person of Jesus, and the love of God displayed at the cross. We see the nearness of God in the life of Jesus, especially when we consider his broken body on the cross. How near was God at that moment? So close that we couldn't begin to comprehend!

In the two natures of Christ—one divine and one human—humanity and divinity are joined forever in the life of Jesus! The powerful revelation that he is near our suffering comes alive when we look at his suffering. Not only do we see the nearness of God, but we see the defeat of death itself. Jesus took away our sins and defeated the enemy.

> **We were not designed to know everything, so turn off that internal switch that strives to be omniscient.**

Even knowing suffering and death were never a part of God's plan. He draws near to us, whispering to our hearts: "It's all gonna be OK."

It was his love that did this—a love manifested through suffering! Wow! This has helped me understand why God's presence feels so real in times of brokenness; it is strongest in the midst of great suffering. This is a great mystery that we can only begin to discover when we gaze at the cross.

You see, the cross changed everything. Not only do we see that God himself suffered so we will no longer suffer, but we know that one day, death—the last enemy—will be defeated for us! That will be the full manifestation of the reality of his nearness.

He will wipe away every tear from their eyes and eliminate death entirely. No one will mourn or weep any longer. The pain of wounds will no longer exist, for the old order has ceased.

REVELATION 21:4 TPT

What a promise! We will have new bodies that are glorified with heavenly tissue and life. This is the Christian hope and faith for our future. His love and presence actually manifest through brokenness and suffering! His love reaches the deepest places of hurt and dark heartache of our souls. Because of the cross, he has already been there. His light has invaded the darkest places, even into death itself. In brokenness, we discover God's love in ways we couldn't otherwise know. This is why the Apostle Paul says:

Rejoice with those who rejoice, weep with those who weep.

ROMANS 12:15 ESV

Beauty in Tears

In harmony with God, our tears become a manifestation of the tears of Jesus, the one who loved us so much that he gave his life for us all. I have experienced this when walking families through the pain of losing a loved one. One family comes to mind. A dear brother had a massive stroke at a young age and went home to be with Jesus. I didn't tell this grieving family that "God must have needed another angel in heaven." Or that "God must have taken him for a reason." What if the reason was that his body was failing? We all have imperfect bodies. Sometimes women have miscarriages; sometimes people get sick; stuff breaks down. God has nothing to do with these causes! They are the direct result of a fallen world.

> **Our tears become a manifestation of the tears of Jesus.**

As I ministered to this dear family, I wept with them, worshiped with them, believed with them. To this day, I love that family with all my heart! When we weep with broken people, our tears become the tears of Jesus. We manifest his tender love and nearness as we capture God's heart for others.

Another time, I was praying for a precious woman who was dying in the hospital. Some of our church family was there along with her husband. We were believing God for her to be healed and walk out of the hospital. I've seen this happen many, many times—even the dead raised—but it did not happen this time.

As we prayed, God manifested his presence in the hospital room. In the midst of this awful suffering, Jesus manifested his peace and love in a tangible way. We wept, not just because this amazing woman of God was coughing up blood, but because of the God she was praising as we prayed. It's hard to convey this awful and powerful moment.

This is why I do not lose my faith through events of suffering. I have seen some amazing miracles in my lifetime, but even when I don't see someone walk out of the hospital after praying for them, I can still see God powerfully near to the broken and suffering ones. God comforts our grieving and mourning; he doesn't cause it!

You're blessed when you feel you've lost what is most dear to you. Only then can you be embraced by the One most dear to you.

MATTHEW 5:4 MSG

I recall a great loss I suffered as a young boy, a time when my innocent heart was broken. Many nights, I cried myself to sleep. Years later, I asked Jesus where he was in those moments of pain. He whispered to my heart: "I was embracing you and weeping with you!" I wept when he said that, but it was a weeping that brought healing. It was so real to me.

He whispered to my heart: "I was embracing you and weeping with you!"

Are you in suffering? It doesn't mean God is far away or unloving. Take comfort in the cross. When we look at the cross, we see the ugliest of sin and the beautiful display of divine love. When we look at suffering, disease, and pain, we see Jesus manifesting his love! Even in mourning, draw from the water that flows from his side and be covered in the precious blood of his suffering. God is with you, even when things happen that are not his heart. Ask Jesus about times in your life that were most painful, and know that he is near to the brokenhearted! He's right there whispering, "Everything is going to be OK!"

We are able to love to the utmost when we know Jesus is near, and he is so near in suffering. Jesus loved the strongest when he suffered the greatest. May that love permeate your entire being, even in your suffering.

The Lord is close to all whose hearts are crushed by pain, and he is always ready to restore the repentant one.
PSALM 34:18 TPT

Before he went to the cross, Jesus' feet were anointed by Mary Magdalene. She drew an expensive fragrance from an alabaster box and wiped his feet with her tears. On the day he died, it is believed that amidst the sweat, the bile, and the blood, that fragrance still hung on his feet. Even his brutal suffering could not remove the scent of the Father's love.

Allow the fragrance of God's love to heal the deep places of your heart's suffering. As you pray, listen to the song "Heaven's Secrets," by Wilder. Remember, Jesus is closer than a brother. A prayer:

Lord, by your sovereign power, straighten this distorted view of you and the way things actually are in the cosmos. In Jesus' name! Amen.

Reflection, Discussion, and Prayer

1. The Bible says God works all things for our good, but it doesn't say he initiates all things. How does that distinction change your relationship with God?

2. In what ways can we partner with God to do his will when it is not being done?

3. Since there is not always some divine reason behind every event, ask God how he will take something broken and make it beautiful. Then, reflect on times he has already done this.

4. In the most broken times of your life, ask Jesus to show you where he was and what he was doing in that moment. Then ask God to help you turn off the internal switch that strives to be omniscient.

CHAPTER EIGHT

LIES, DAMN LIES, AND INSIGNIFICANCE

The amazing grace of the Master, Jesus Christ, the extravagant love of God, the intimate friendship of the Holy Spirit, be with all of you.

2 CORINTHIANS 13:14 MSG

M Y TEENAGE YEARS IN Las Vegas, Nevada were quite the adventure. I was born in Denver, Colorado and moved to Las Vegas when I was twelve years old. Being a teenager is challenging enough, but I was a teenager in "Sin City." For a few years, I lived within walking distance from the strip, the place where all the crazy stuff happens. Tourists go to party like there's no tomorrow. *What happens in Vegas, stays in Vegas.* With the possible exception of hangovers, gambling debt, and broken marriages.

Imagine brilliant hotels, posh resorts, flashing casinos, and a mass of people absorbed by hedonist pursuits. You get the picture. It was easy for a sixteen-year-old to buy beer. Just pay a homeless guy to use his I.D. Drugs were also plentiful in the atmosphere of "anything goes." Indeed, it went.

When my friends and I were not outdoing each other at partying, we were looking for an adrenaline rush. It was the classic quandry: "What to do after you get stoned?" In Vegas, opportunities abounded. Sometimes it was vandalizing a hotel or casino—until they caught us and threw us out. At one point, I faced arrest if I entered ten different properties.

One night, we decided to forgo the game of evading security guards, and instead, break our own record for stupidity. A friend lived in a one-story house on a golf course. As one of the older communities in Las Vegas, it was adorned with mature trees with spreading limbs. Our brilliant idea was to swing from the roof to roof using those branches, Tarzan style. Unfortunately, Jane wasn't there to scream: "What are you thinking?"

We couldn't find any rope, so in a flash of ingenuity, we grabbed an old water hose, made sure it could support us, and just for good measure, duct taped the worn spots. As if this wasn't exhilarating enough, we decided to swing over the neighbor's fence—a white metal structure crowned with six-inch spikes, most likely to deter invaders. To a naive teenager without beer money, this plan presented untold excitement. Challenge accepted!

> **I lay on my back, certain of a broken neck, thankful to have missed the deadly spikes.**

When it was my turn, I swung off the roof towards the fence. Just as I cleared the spikes, however, the hose snapped. *Oh, snap!* What happened next played out in slow-motion. I imagined myself landing on the spikes with one through my chest. I'd bleed out on that fence, telling my bros to smoke a joint for me and pour beer on the ground on which I died. (I watched a lot of movies.)

Obviously, that's not what happened. Somehow, the momentum of the swing flipped me upside down, slammed me on my head as my back struck the fence and slid to the ground.

I lay on my back, certain of a broken neck, thankful to have missed the deadly spikes. My stoned friends, on the other hand, pointed at me and laughed. What is it about teenagers that they find hilarity in someone's misfortune? Of course, I'd laughed at my friends' predicaments countless times when they wiped out doing something dumb and dangerous. But prostrate on that hard ground, counting my limbs and terrified, I was having none of it. "Bros, I almost died. It's not funny!" Of course, this only elicited more laughter.

Realizing I'd get no help from this gang, I rolled over and tried to walk away. That's when my worst fears seized me. I couldn't move. Now, dying, I could live with. (Don't try to figure that out.) But a paraplegic? Visions of wheelchairs, hospital beds, nurses in crisp white uniforms flooded my mind.

Just as quickly, I realized the problem. During the fall, instead of breaking my neck or being impaled on the spikes, I broke my big toe! I had broken other bones before, but this was different. It wasn't a trip to the doctor for an x-ray and cast. I couldn't walk. I spent weeks on crutches, relying on other people for mundane tasks that I'd always taken for granted. From breaking one little part of the body, I was an invalid.

Toe-tally Significant

What's the point of this story? Well, it's about not being a stupid teenager—at any age! Good luck with that! Really though, there is much more to learn. Have you ever felt that God loved you, but you didn't seem to fit in anywhere? Have you ever felt insignificant, unimportant, trivial? I'm sure we all have. Maybe you feel that way right now.

Soon after my conversion and call to ministry, we started the church in Las Vegas, and God reminded me of this story. *What's the significance, Lord?* It all made sense after reading a passage from 1 Corinthians. Now, before you jump ahead, allow me to give you some context. This is vital when interpreting Scripture. Many people make the Bible say whatever they want it to say. I want you to get the truth.

In the first century, Christianity was growing in regions beyond Jerusalem. The Gentile nations were responding to the gospel and experiencing God's love, but their cultures did not share the Jewish heritage forged under the Law. The Gentiles were rebellious and oppressed by sin. One region in particular was known as crazy and wild; that was the Church at Corinth. Paul's ministry to this bunch required detailed instructions on common civility and morality. His biggest challenge, however, was getting them to get along as a community. So, Paul taught them the beautiful mystery of people's lives connected in the Christian community. He called it the Body of Christ, and he used an analogy of the human body to illustrate the workings of this marvelous organization.

Let's read 1 Corinthians 12:12-14 in the Message.

You can easily enough see how this kind of thing works by looking no further than your own body. Your body has many parts—limbs, organs, cells—but no matter how many parts you can name, you're still one body. It's exactly the same with Christ. By means of his one Spirit, we all said good-bye to our partial and piecemeal lives. We each used to independently call our own shots, but then we entered into a large and integrated life in which he has the final say in everything. (This is what we proclaimed in word and action when we were baptized.) Each of us is now a part of his resurrection body, refreshed and sustained at one fountain—his Spirit—where we all come to drink. The old labels we once used to identify ourselves— labels like Jew or Greek, slave or free—are no longer useful. We need something larger, more comprehensive.

I want you to think about how all this makes you more significant, not less.

I want you to think about how all this makes you more significant, not less. A body isn't just a single part blown up

into something huge. It's all the different-but-similar parts
arranged and functioning together.

1 CORINTHIANS 12:12-14 MSG

Wow! Paul is communicating something so vital, so needed, not just for the new believers at Corinth but for believers everywhere. These verses gripped me when I began pastoring the new church in Las Vegas. We attracted people from all walks of life: drug addicts, drug dealers, prostitutes, pimps, broken bodies, corrupt spirits, destitute souls. This was King David in the cave of Adullam with his band of outcasts and misfits. They were messed up, but they saw God's anointing on David, and they chose to follow him, even to a cave. I knew exactly how David felt.

This powerful truth, so profound, changed how I approached ministry. Look again at verse 14:

I want you to think about how all this makes you more sig-
nificant, not less. A body isn't just a single part blown up
into something huge. It's all the different-but-similar parts
arranged and functioning together.

The Lie of Insignificance

It all made sense to me in that moment. Every part of the Body of Christ is significant. Even a stinky toe! Before I broke my toe, I didn't realize its importance to my mobility. Likewise, we don't appreciate our significance within the community of Christ or relationships in general. Paul was not merely trying to get the Corinthians to be a healthy church. He was telling them that in this great mystery called the Body of Christ, every part is significant. Not just those who seem more important than others. Not just those up front or behind a pulpit. Not just those wearing a robe or speaking to the masses. If one part fails, no matter how seemingly insignificant, the whole body suffers. In our age of instant fame and superstardom, it's easy to feel insignificant to the Body of Christ. There is a deep root in the hearts of God's people that hinders them from the freedom to be who they are in Christ. It is the lie of insignificance.

Our significance determines our value system. It's the connection between how an individual thinks of themselves, and how they function in life. Knowing our true significance changes the way we see everything:

- the way we see ourselves
- the way we see loved ones
- the way we see the bride/body of Christ
- the way we see unbelievers
- the way we function in every relationship

Basing our value systems on a community that exalts gifting, title, or position can be toxic. This is why many people struggle to know their true value and significance in relationships and community.

As God's kids, however, our significance should be rooted in his love. Striving for significance in our titles, positions, giftings, or a platform takes us away from this love. These value systems present themselves in different ways . . . if we are honest. It shows our narcissism and the self-centered way we do life, church, and relationships. Even our desire to be seen—which is our reaction to feeling invisible—is connected to self-promotion. *You know, we gotta get to the next level!* When I hear this in church, I want to scream: "What the heck is the next level, anyway?" It's one of those terms we should drop, along with our titles.

Notice, I did not say lay aside our functions. We can still walk

> There is a deep root in the hearts of God's people that hinders them from the freedom to be who they are in Christ. It is the lie of insignificance.

in the grace of God without a title. I don't like when someone is forced to "honor" a leader by using some long title. (By the way, I'm now known as Bishop Apostle Senior Leader Pastor Zackary Wechsler.) Am I making fun of titles? Well, yes . . . and no. I'm exposing the flattering value system behind them. Once we learn our significance without them, then maybe we can start using them again . . . in moderation! In the meantime, just call me Zack.

Changing Our Culture

May the love of God drive a light sword through this junk. May we learn the difference between honor and flattery. If you are surrounded by those who insist on titles, especially by leaders who don't function in the title they claim, I suggest you find some new friends.

> Insecure leaders control others, and insecure people call out leaders for being controlling because they want that title or position.

These toxic value systems are evident in the fear-based ways some people control their environment, both in leadership roles and non-leadership roles. Fearing loss of position, prestige, or promotion, they hold on for dear life. Why? Because it's the only thing that makes them feel important. They can't imagine life without that false significance. Clearly, they have missed it. We cannot find true significance apart from the love of God. Anything else corrupts the way we do life. Insecure leaders control others, and insecure people call out leaders for being controlling because they want that title or position. Lord have mercy on us all! Church folk be on Jerry Springer too!

This is what Paul dealt with in Corinth. He stressed that every part of the body is significant. You don't have to search for your value; you just have to know it. Even the sensitive parts you keep hidden (I'll leave the rest to your imagination) are actually more important, not less. That means the person on the back row who loves to come in unnoticed is no less important than the lady who prophesizes up front every Sunday.

Early in my pastoral ministry, as this powerful truth revolutionized my life, ministry, and message, my heart began to ache for all those who don't fit in, as well as those so wrapped up in position, gifting, and title that they got high on their own fumes. They couldn't see past their eyeballs unless something was in it for them. I must admit, I have struggled with both of these attitudes and probably everything in between. Life is a great learning experience.

Our value systems must change. That's why I'm bringing to light the broken and neglected big toes of the church. I call forth the stinky feet! We must realize how God's amazing love impacts our relationships and callings. It affects how we function, how we are known, and how we know others in the community. God loves community. That doesn't just mean he loves all of us. We know he loves us individually, but his heart and design for us is to be in a community. We all need family. Church community is not some corporate structure with CEO's, managers, and subordinates all fighting for personalized parking. The church is a place we can call home and experience family. It's where we find love, where we discover who we are and what we are designed for. It's where we become fully alive.

> **Church is a gift of sacred community. Yet we must first receive it, and then unwrap it.**

Church is a gift of sacred community. Yet we must first receive it, and then unwrap it. For most of us, however, community means relationships, and relationships harken past pain. Trust me, I know. One of my calls in life is to help people with church-related wounds. Church wounding is not one-sided, by the way. It's not just shepherds hurting sheep. We also have sheep hurting shepherds. I have personally experienced both sides of rejection, betrayal, and heartaches.

There are broken toes throughout the body of Christ that need to be healed. There are parts of the body that we have belittled or ignored, yet they are more vital than the visible parts. Of course, all of this doesn't just apply to a church but to the community in general. This includes all of humanity and every person knowing their true significance.

> Systems of striving, competition, and flattery are changing as we see one another through the lens of God's scandalous love.

The word *honor* has become a Christian cliche. Do we know what honor is? I find myself trying to honor people and really, I'm just flattering them. We don't need fresh bandages for these seeping scars. We need healing.

The revelation of our significance lays an axe to the root. It shouts loudly at the fruitless fig tree: "WITHER!" Value systems that don't bear fruit are being exposed. Systems of striving, competition, and flattery are changing as we see one another through the lens of God's scandalous love. That's honor—to see and value one another through the lens of love.

True honor and significance cultivate gifts of which we never dreamed. Flattery feeds a false sense of self. It identifies us beyond our true calling, trapping us into striving to become what we believe others think we are. It is motivated by titles, platforms, pomp, and positions. Honor is motivated by the love of the Father revealing our significance to him apart from our gifts and talents.

I love to see people who know their significance, not just alone but within a healthy community. Our value systems must change. And the only way to do that correctly is through the scandalous love of God. No wonder many feel that something is missing. We need a reformation! I believe God is raising up reformers today who are humble servants of our loving God, people who don't operate in fear-based leadership styles. They wash feet like Jesus did, and they love people into their significance. We come alive when we discover our true value. We stop striving for the next level or title. We flip the script and discover beautiful people around us, people who are significant because of God's love.

Brick by Brick

Here's a test. If our gifts, titles, positions, and anointing were stripped from us, how significant would we feel? If that's a hard question, take heart. The church is changing, reforming, and rising from the toxic cultures of her past. God is loving the crap out of us! Rather than criticize the lack, become the more!

It's amazing how God teaches us significance through relationship, family, and church community. Such a beautiful process! In our Las Vegas church, people discovered their significance through Scripture, in worship, or at a table with friends. We saw it all! It changed their lives and affected the entire body.

Love is centered on others; it is self-giving and willing to sacrifice.

It was amazing to watch a community form. God built a temple for his love to inhabit. He used us, as living stones. On this road to discovering our significance, we simply received God's love, and that love overflowed to others.

Love is centered on others; it is self-giving and willing to sacrifice. In families or church communities, people learn to love deeply and serve one another. As we are baptized in his love, we see the significance of every person through the eyes of heaven.

God has a gift for you. It's a loving community, a family, a place where you find your significance along with others. It's a body arranged to function in self-giving love. You may not have found this gift of community. Or maybe it's right in front of you but you haven't embraced it. It's in receiving this sacred community—a vivid expression of Trinitarian love—that we learn to walk in true identity, not a solo act but a symphony, a song of love for a broken world, drawing it to wholeness.

Love in Action

Here's a story of how significance played out for our family.

We had the honor of sharing our family with a young man in our church, Larris. He is so special to us. When we first met Larris, he was a rebellious teenager getting into trouble and lacking direction for his life. He surrendered his life to Jesus in our youth group and started serving in the community. He became a son to Rachelle and me, and he lived with us for five years. It was a blessing for him to have his own room and be a part of our family, but we were the ones honored to have him in our lives. He ate at our table, played with his new brothers and sisters, and saw us in our low times and high times. To this day, I have a hole in my heart that only Larris can fill.

Today, Larris is married, working, going to college, serving in church, and on track for a wonderful career. His life was transformed by God through community, family, and knowing his own significance. His life was transformed by the scandalous love of God.

What a picture of how God, as Father, Son, and Holy Spirit, has welcomed us into the shared life of the Trinity! Just like this awesome young man, Larris, you also have been chosen for significance.

Come to the table. Come home.

Reflection, Discussion, and Prayer

1. Since every human being has significance, and every part of a church or family is significant, how can you receive the gift of your community / family around you? How does community / family help you feel known and loved by God?

2. Ask God to show you some of the lies you believe that lead you to think you are insignificant. Then ask him to tell you how loved you are without a position, gift, talent, or platform.

3. Pause and reflect on the difference between flattery and honor. Think of ways to practically honor / value people in your life.

4. Like the story of Larris, sometimes we live from a place of not knowing our significance. But being surrounded by loving people changes that. Ask God to show you those people in your life who need to be surrounded and valued.

CHAPTER NINE

HALF DEAD AND BLEEDING OUT

"Finally, another man, a Samaritan, came upon the bleeding man and was moved with tender compassion for him. He stooped down and gave him first aid, pouring olive oil on his wounds, disinfecting them with wine, and bandaging them to stop the bleeding. Lifting him up, he placed him on his own donkey and brought him to an inn. Then he took him from his donkey and carried him to a room for the night. The next morning he took his own money from his wallet and gave it to the innkeeper with these words: 'Take care of him until I come back from my journey. If it costs more than this, I will repay you when I return.' So, now, tell me, which one of the three men who saw the wounded man proved to be the true neighbor?"

The religious scholar responded, "The one who demonstrated kindness and mercy."

Jesus said, "You must go and do the same as he."

LUKE 10:33-37 TPT

HAVE YOU EVER WATCHED a movie and thought: *I'm that person in the story?* I do this all the time, especially when the guy is tough and good looking. As a kid, I'd tell

117

my friends: "I'm Superman, Batman, and Spiderman all in one!" Nowadays, I'd make a great stand-in for Thor.

We do the same thing with Bible stories. In Luke 10, Jesus told a parable after being asked a question by a religious scholar. It's the familiar story of the good Samaritan, and it comes from a place in the gospels that teaches benevolence and compassion for broken people. I love that concept. The church—the people of God—should be showing the world what true love is. I preach this message all the time and try to live it to the best of my ability.

Now, the good Samaritan parable is usually taught from the perspective of the Samaritan himself. And that's who we are in the story—the good guy or gal, the superhero, the one who saves the day. Because that's what Christians do . . . right?

Well, yes, but is that what we should assume in this story? Are we reading it correctly? Or are we viewing it through a religious lens? We are going to look at this story a bit differently, and I promise it will shift your paradigm of God's love.

For context, let's start at the beginning of the conversation between Jesus and this expert in the law.

Just then a religious scholar stood before Jesus in order to test his doctrines. He posed this question: "Teacher, what requirement must I fulfill if I want to live forever in heaven?"

Jesus replied, "What does Moses teach us? What do you read in the Law?"

The religious scholar answered, "It states, 'You must love the Lord God with all your heart, all your passion, all your energy, and your every thought. And you must love your neighbor as well as you love yourself.'"

Jesus said, "That is correct. Now go and do exactly that and you will live."

Wanting to justify himself, he questioned Jesus further, saying, "What do you mean by 'my neighbor'?"

LUKE 10:25-29 TPT

I love how Jesus answers the religious scholar's question with another question.

Jesus replied, "What does Moses teach us? What do you read in the Law?"

Isn't that like the Lord? He led the scholar into answering his own question with Scripture:

The religious scholar answered, "It states, 'You must love the Lord God with all your heart, all your passion, all your energy, and your every thought. And you must love your neighbor as well as you love yourself.'"

Hold on! *All your passion? All your energy? Every thought?* When was the last time you went a whole day without an imperfect thought before God? *Hmmm let me think about it. . . . . Ah, never mind.*

It's as if Jesus wanted the scholar to speak this passage so he would really think it through.

> **The religious scholar built his own coffin, and Jesus nailed it shut with one deft stroke.**

Is it really possible to do this perfectly? I can hear the crowd of onlookers chuckling: "Good luck with that one, buddy!"

In quoting the law accurately, the religious scholar built his own coffin, and Jesus nailed it shut with one deft stroke.

"That is correct. Now go and do exactly that and you will live."

Go and do! He told the scholar if he wants to go to heaven, he has to obey the law perfectly. *Do exactly what you said and you'll live.* Nice if he could. He'd take a little credit. Inflate his chest. But that's the point, isn't it? Who can keep the law? No one but Jesus. So, why do we read the story with this same self-righteous lens?

Exposed by the truth, the scholar struggled to stay afloat. We do the same, rationalizing our good and bad behavior, trying to look good to those around us and stay in God's love. The scholar was down to one desperate shot, so he took aim at Jesus' definitions:

"What do you mean by 'my neighbor'?"

Thus began the famous parable of the good Samaritan. Watch closely.

Jesus replied, "Listen and I will tell you. — There was once a Jewish man traveling from Jerusalem to Jericho when bandits robbed him along the way. They beat him severely, stripped him naked, and left him half dead."

Now, the road from Jerusalem to Jericho was a treacherous passage. Descending from 2000 feet to below sea level, it earned the title: "the bloody road." Still, many traveled it. It was a common highway, the unavoidable journey of life.

Soon, a Jewish priest walking down the same road came upon the wounded man. Seeing him from a distance, the priest crossed to the other side of the road and walked right past him, not turning to help him one bit.

The Jewish priest is an allegory for how we exalt the law above love and substitute our religious efforts for the heart of God. The priest didn't want to get near the fallen man because he didn't want to be defiled. How many times do we distance ourselves from broken people, thinking to keep ourselves unsoiled?

Later, a religious man, a Levite, came walking down the same road and likewise crossed to the other side to pass by the wounded man without stopping to help him.

The Levite was a slave to fear, and it dictated his actions.

Finally, another man, a Samaritan, came upon the bleeding man and was moved with tender compassion for him.

This is where most people project themselves as the good guy in the story. Of course, I agree we should aspire to be loving to broken people—absolutely. But we need to ask: Who is Jesus in the story? After all, we can't really know our place until we know God's place.

The Scandalous Samaritan

Further, who is this Samaritan? Samaritans were despised as half-breeds; they were not considered covenant people by the Jews. They were a mixed-race people from when Jews intermingled with Assyrians (721 BC). Thus, they were not pure to those with a religious mindset. When the Jews dis-

> Who is Jesus in the story? After all, we can't really know our place until we know God's place.

paraged Jesus by calling him a Samaritan in John 8:48, they were implying that he was a half-breed, born of an unfaithful mother. (It's a wonder Jesus didn't nuke them on the spot.) So, even Jesus calling the Samaritan "good" in this story was scandalous.

What if the Samaritan in the story was a description of Christ and his love? This is not commonly taught today, but many of our church fathers (e.g., Origen, Ambrose, and Augustine) affirmed that the Samaritan is a symbol of Christ. For example, the Samaritan was moved with tender compassion for the wounded man. Was not our Lord constantly moved with compassion upon the multitudes? What did the Samaritan do when he found the wounded man?

He stooped down and gave him first aid . . .

Paul, in Philippians 2, says that Jesus humbled himself.

> *He existed in the form of God, yet he gave no thought to seizing equality with God as his supreme prize. Instead he emptied himself of his outward glory by reducing himself to the form of a lowly servant. He became human! He humbled himself and became vulnerable, choosing to be revealed as a man and was obedient. He was a perfect example, even in his death—a criminal's death by crucifixion!*
>
> PHILIPPIANS 2:6-8 TPT

We are the wounded man, bleeding out and left for dead.

I submit that we are not the good Samaritan; Jesus is! So, who are we? We are the wounded man, bleeding out and left for dead. Of course, we should aspire to the qualities of the Samaritan, but look at the evidence of our identity in this parable:

- We bear the wounds of sin.
- We cannot save ourselves.
- We are traveling the difficult journey of life.
- We are bound to fall into some sort of trouble.
- We cannot be saved by self-effort or religion.
- We have been beaten down, robbed, and left for dead.
- We are hopeless.

Before we can truly represent the life of Christ, we must realize our need for healing and freedom through the scandalous love of God.

Notice how the Samaritan treated the broken man.

He stooped down and gave him first aid, pouring olive oil on his wounds, disinfecting them with wine, and bandaging them to stop the bleeding.

Is this not the ministry of the Holy Spirit? Cleansing with wine being the blood of Jesus Christ? Bandaging the bleeding, emulating the Father's healing embrace?

Interestingly, the original language describes the sequence as bandaging the wounds, then pouring oil and wine on it. This seems backwards. Why wouldn't the Samaritan clean the wound and then bandage it? Well, some wounds are so deep, they must be bound first to stop the bleeding! This is truly an illustration of "come as you are!" But of course, not

> **Some wounds are so deep, they must be bound first to stop the bleeding!**

"stay as you are." Deep wounds can only be healed through the embrace of our loving Papa, God the Father!

Lifting him up, he placed him on his own donkey and brought him to an inn. Then he took him from his donkey and carried him to a room for the night.

Are we not lifted up with Christ, as Paul says in Ephesians 2:6 (TPT)?

He raised us up with Christ, the exalted One, and we ascended with him into the glorious perfection and authority of the heavenly realm, for we are now co-seated as one with Christ!

123

The Samaritan placed the man on his own donkey and brought him to an inn. Was not Jesus our substitute? Woah! This changes everything. This is scandalous to the religious mind and shocking to the broken sinner. The good Samaritan is not just some folk hero we should emulate. He's the scandalous love of God in action, the good news of Jesus and how he redeems all of us!

The next morning he took his own money from his wallet and gave it to the innkeeper with these words: "Take care of him until I come back from my journey. If it costs more than this, I will repay you when I return."

We see the Trinity once again—the innkeeper as the Father and Jesus leaving the Holy Spirit as a down payment on our redemption. Paul echoes this in Ephesians.

Now we have been stamped with the seal of the promised Holy Spirit. He is given to us like an engagement ring, as the first installment of what's coming!

EPHESIANS 1:13-14 TPT

Lastly, we have this assurance of the Samaritan's return for the wounded man.

Take care of him until I come back from my journey. If it costs more than this, I will repay you when I return.

Will not Jesus return in glory? Has he not paid all? Most certainly he has and he will.

New Eyes to See the Dawn

Allow your eyes to open to a new paradigm, revealing a greater depth of the Father's love. It's staggering. It's scandalous. It's ancient truth awakening the church. It's the gospel.

124

Jesus did as much to the religious scholar laid bare before him. Stripped of religion, he was finally open to truth. In this teachable moment, Jesus delivered the final word with devastating accuracy.

"So, now, tell me, which one of the three men who saw the wounded man proved to be the true neighbor?"

The religious scholar responded, "The one who demonstrated kindness and mercy."

Jesus said, "You must go and do the same as he."

Point. Set. Match.

If the Samaritan is Jesus, then the message is clear: the scholar's only hope is to follow Jesus. All followers of Jesus must trust in him completely. Our salvation is not a religious effort or good behavior. God's scandalous love nullifies even our best deeds. As the hymn says: "Our hope is built on nothing less, than Jesus' blood and righteousness."

> **God's scandalous love nullifies even our best deeds.**

I love what Jesus says in Matthew 11:

Are you tired? Worn out? Burned out on religion? Come to me. Get away with me and you'll recover your life. I'll show you how to take a real rest. Walk with me and work with me—watch how I do it. Learn the unforced rhythms of grace. I won't lay anything heavy or ill-fitting on you. Keep company with me and you'll learn to live freely and lightly.
MATTHEW 11:28-30 MSG

The unforced rhythms of grace. Grace is a rhythm you can't force. You can only yield to it. Don't be like people who dance funny at weddings, especially those with CRD—Caucasian

Rhythm Disorder. We can't force the Christian life. We must learn the unforced rhythms of grace and join with the Triune God in the dance of love. Remember that Greek word *perichoresis*? It describes the relationship of the Trinity—the divine dance. As we receive this grace, we participate in the joy, love, and life of the triune God.

There is an icon from the 15th century called "The Trinity" (or "The Hospitality of Abraham") painted by Andrei Rublev. It depicts the story of the three angels Abraham entertained in Genesis 18. In the icon, you can see clearly that Andrei Rublev made a space at the table with the three angels that represent the Trinity. You and I are invited to fellowship with God himself into this beautiful, mysterious divine dance with him.

There's a place for us at Jesus' wedding. We'll be the ones in white. And we'll dance a new dance, one in perfect harmony with the Father, Son, and Holy Spirit.

So come and feast. You are invited to the table—you who are hungry and hopeless, bleeding and dying. Accept Jesus as he kneels to rescue you. Trust him. Follow the rhythm of divine grace and join in the dance. As you contemplate and pray, I dare you to look up the song "We Dance," by Steffany Gretzinger.

Get wrecked by God's scandalous love as you dance the dance of eternal lovers.

Reflection, Discussion, and Prayer

1. Our religious practices do not save us, and neither do our behavior modifications. How does this change the way you see the depths of Gods scandalous love?

2. Learning that the Samaritan is a type of Christ as we are on this unavoidable journey of life, how has Jesus stooped down and saved you when you were unable to save yourself?

3. Some wounds are so deep that before they can be disinfected, they must be bound with bandages. Describe how the Father has shown you this kind of love right where you are.

4. Ask God to show you how you can yield to the unforced rhythms of grace and live the life he intended.

CHAPTER TEN

THE ABBA OF JESUS

And not many days after, the younger son gathered all together, journeyed to a far country, and there wasted his possessions with prodigal living.

LUKE 15:13 NKJV

OUR VIEW OF GOD determines how we view ourselves. This is why, in previous chapters, we've discussed how:

+ God reaches into our dark places of brokenness and hiding.
+ God chose us, speaking to us in our conflict.
+ God empowers us to rise up.
+ God gives us our real identity.
+ God says we are significant apart from what we do.
+ God does not control everything that happens to us.
+ God's scandalous love makes us free.

Everything we've examined is vital to living as God intended us to live. And yet . . . there's more. It is vital that we realize the primary work of the Holy Spirit in our lives. It's not what you may think.

While most churches are open to the Holy Spirit to a degree, the charismatic church is a form of Christianity that emphasizes the work of the Holy Spirit and spiritual gifts. It is a culture that believes in the gifts of the Holy Spirit as described in 1 Corinthians 12. Yet churches that believe in the Spirit-filled life often get a bad rap. Of the hundreds of millions of charismatic Christians in the Body of Christ, most are mature believers of a holy God. Unfortunately, it's the fringes of the charismatic church that become the face of the movement. The biggest weakness I see is when churches limit the work of the Holy Spirit to outward manifestations: a worship experience, speaking in tongues, prophecy, healing, etc.

Don't get me wrong. The spiritual gifts are wonderful. Every Christian can and should have them operating in their life. These gifts were designed to build up the body of Christ. "Now to each one the manifestation of the Spirit is given for the common good" (1 Cor. 12:7 NIV). We need everything God offers to us. He equips us for a reason.

Yet it's important to realize that the Holy Spirit is not just some force that gives us goosebumps in church. The Holy Spirit is the third person of the Godhead. Jesus said the Holy Spirit is the Spirit of truth. Jesus promised that he would not leave us orphans, but that he would give us the Holy Spirit. Further, the Holy Spirit would honor him, guiding us into all truth, taking what is his [Jesus'] and giving it to us.

> *If you love Me, keep My commandments. And I will pray to the Father, and He will give you another Helper, that He may abide with you forever—the Spirit of truth, whom the world cannot receive, because it neither sees Him nor knows Him; but you know Him, for He dwells with you and will be in you. I will not leave you orphans; I will come to you.*
>
> JOHN 14:15-18 NKJV

> *I still have many things to tell you, but you can't handle them now. But when the Friend comes, the Spirit of the Truth, he will take you by the hand and guide you into*

all the truth there is. He won't draw attention to himself, but will make sense out of what is about to happen and, indeed, out of all that I have done and said. He will honor me; he will take from me and deliver it to you. Everything the Father has is also mine. That is why I've said, "He takes from me and delivers to you."

JOHN 16:12-15 MSG

Notice that Jesus described the Holy Spirit differently than mere outward expressions. Despite Jesus' teaching, however, people often do things that they attribute to the Holy Spirit, but these acts draw more attention to themselves than to God. This is in contrast to Jesus' teaching that the Holy Spirit would not draw attention to himself. So, if we're doing something that attracts attention to ourselves (or others), and we're calling it the Holy Spirit, maybe it's not a pure manifestation of the Holy Spirit.

> If we're doing something that attracts attention to ourselves (or others), and we're calling it the Holy Spirit, maybe it's not a pure manifestation of the Holy Spirit.

Paul said in 1 Corinthians 12 that the Holy Spirit will always exalt Jesus as Lord. So, if an outward expression of spiritual manifestation doesn't glorify Jesus, we have reason to question it.

Making God's Fatherhood Real

The Holy Spirit's primary work is to point us to Jesus, and Jesus always reveals the heart of the Father. It looks like this:

1. We receive the Holy Spirit.
2. The Holy Spirit reveals Jesus.
3. Jesus reveals the Father.

Consider what Paul says about the work of the Spirit:

The mature children of God are those who are moved by the impulses of the Holy Spirit. And you did not receive the "spirit of religious duty," leading you back into the fear of never being good enough. But you have received the "Spirit of full acceptance," enfolding you into the family of God. And you will never feel orphaned, for as he rises up within us, our spirits join him in saying the words of tender affection, "Beloved Father!" For the Holy Spirit makes God's fatherhood real to us as he whispers into our innermost being, "You are God's beloved child!"

ROMANS 8:14-16 TPT

The Holy Spirit confirms deep within us that we are children of God. He is the Spirit of adoption. He is not a spirit of fear, religious duty, or bondage. The Holy Spirit witnesses to us that we are fully loved and accepted in the family of God. Until we grasp this truth, our outward expressions of the Holy Spirit will be immature and misguided.

> **The primary work of the Spirit is to help us understand, deep within us, that we are beloved sons and daughters.**

Look at this passage again:

The Holy Spirit makes God's fatherhood real to us as he whispers into our innermost being, "You are God's beloved child!"

The primary work of the Spirit isn't to give us a little bit of fire in our prayer life. It's not to give us some special gifts. Yes, that's part of it, but the primary work of the Spirit is to help us understand, deep within us, that we are beloved sons and daughters. This is the beautiful work of the Holy Spirit in us and through us.

Let's read this powerful Scripture in The Message Bible.

This resurrection life you received from God is not a timid, grave-tending life. It's adventurously expectant, greeting God with a childlike "What's next, Papa?" God's Spirit touches our spirits and confirms who we really are. We know who he is, and we know who we are: Father and children. And we know we are going to get what's coming to us—an unbelievable inheritance! We go through exactly what Christ goes through. If we go through the hard times with him, then we're certainly going to go through the good times with him!

ROMANS 8:14-16 MSG

Wow! So the Holy Spirit confirms who we really are. When we know who he is, we discover who we are.

And so that we would know for sure that we are his true children, God released the Spirit of Sonship into our hearts—moving us to cry out intimately, "My Father! You're our true Father!"

GALATIANS 4:6 TPT

This is why the apostle Paul encourages Timothy to fan the flame in his heart, to stir up the gift within him:

I think of your strong faith that was passed down through your family line. It began with your grandmother Lois, who passed it on to your dear mother, Eunice. And it's clear that you too are following in the footsteps of their godly example.

I'm writing to encourage you to fan into a flame and rekindle the fire of the spiritual gift God imparted to you when I laid my hands upon you.

2 TIMOTHY 1:5-6 TPT

What is this fire that Paul is speaking of? What is this gift?

It is the Holy Spirit. It is a reminder to stir up the fire of God's love within him. Yes, Paul was acknowledging Timothy's genuine faith, but he was also telling him to stir up another part of his faith—the fiery love of God. It is the deep work of the Spirit that reminds Timothy of who he is.

Let me demonstrate this to you. Paul opens the letter addressing Timothy as: "My beloved son."

From Paul, an apostle of Jesus the Messiah, appointed by God's pleasure to announce the wonderful promise of life found in Jesus, the anointed Messiah.

My beloved son, I pray for a greater release of God's grace, love, and total well-being to flow into your life from God our Father and from our Lord Jesus Christ!

2 TIMOTHY 1:1-2 TPT

In referring to Timothy as a beloved son, Paul doesn't mention Timothy's biological father. It's not clear if his dad was a believer, but clearly Paul sees Timothy as a spiritual son. It is beautiful to see the love of the Father expressed through the Apostle Paul. The solid love of the Father must be the foundation of every ministry. Without it, we are building on shifting sand, exposed to the winds and rain, destined for destruction.

In the original language, *my beloved son* is the same phrase the Father spoke over Jesus when he emerged from the waters of baptism.

When He had been baptized, Jesus came up immediately from the water; and behold, the heavens were opened to Him, and He saw the Spirit of God descending like a dove and alighting upon Him. And suddenly a voice came from heaven, saying, "This is My beloved Son, in whom I am well pleased."

MATTHEW 3:16-17 NKJV

By calling Timothy "my beloved son," Paul was conveying the Father's voice, affirming that Timothy was a beloved son of Father God, who was well pleased with him. No wonder Paul encouraged Timothy not to neglect the gift that was in him nor despise his youth. Paul was affirming him, encouraging him to be who he was created to be, and that all started with knowing he was a beloved child of God. Paul then elaborated on the nature of this Spirit of adoption.

For God has not given us a spirit of fear, but of power and of love and of a sound mind.

2 TIMOTHY 1:7 NKJV

Paul's term: *spirit of fear,* is echoed in his letter to the Romans:

For you did not receive the spirit of bondage again to fear, but you received the Spirit of adoption by whom we cry out, "Abba, Father."

ROMANS 8:15 NKJV

Adoption is the deep work of the Holy Spirit in our lives. It is the bedrock upon which every other gift is built. Knowing we are beloved sons and daughters is key to walking in the power of the Holy Spirit. This is why we should never limit the work of the Holy Spirit to supernatural experiences or gifts. As the life-giving Spirit of God, his primary role is to teach us to cry "Abba, Father."

> Adoption is the deep work of the Holy Spirit in our lives. It is the bedrock upon which every other gift is built.

As a minister, I have seen people drenched in the love of God, weeping as I preach this particular portion of the gospels. There is a great healing presence of God in these words. That same healing oil is flowing for you, my reader. It doesn't matter how long you have been a Christian. If you feel separated from God's love, if you think you are the rottenest sinner on earth, prepare to discover a greater revelation of the Father's love.

An Abba Like No Other

In Luke 15, Jesus told a story of the prodigal son. The youngest son demanded his inheritance so he could set out in life. There is more to this than the obvious. In the 1st century, asking for an inheritance while your father was alive was tantamount to saying, "You're dead to me, Dad. I want what's coming to me now!"

Can you imagine the father's grief in that moment? *You're dead to me.* It must have devastated him. But he let his son go anyway. The young man went to a far country and lived like a hedonist until his money ran out. He ended up feeding pigs and stealing their food to survive. Today, he'd have gone to Vegas, spent all his money drinking himself into the gutter and woken up fighting rats for restaurant scraps.

It was at this point that the youngest son realized he could have a better life as one of his father's servants. So he formed a plan.

But when he came to himself, he said, "How many of my father's hired servants have bread enough and to spare, and I perish with hunger! I will arise and go to my father, and will say to him, 'Father, I have sinned against heaven and before you, and I am no longer worthy to be called your son. Make me like one of your hired servants.'"

LUKE 15:17-19 NKJV

But love had other ideas for this returning prodigal.

And he arose and came to his father. But when he was still a great way off, his father saw him and had compassion, and ran and fell on his neck and kissed him.

LUKE 15:20 NKJV

Now, we have to know something of the culture in this day. Older men did not run; it was disrespectful, even scandalous, if you will. Therefore, in telling this parable, Jesus was stretching the limits of how a good father behaves. But there was a purpose in this; Jesus was describing the extravagant love of the Father for all of us.

Notice how the prodigal's father saw him from "a great way off." Obviously, the father had been searching the horizon, yearning for his son to come home. We see the Father's heart as he greeted him with kisses of love and forgiveness.

I love this quote by Brennan Manning in *The Furious Longing of God.*

> **Older men did not run; it was disrespectful, even scandalous.**

If you took the love of all the best mothers and fathers who have lived in the course of human history, all their goodness, kindness, patience, fidelity, wisdom, tenderness, strength, and love and united all those qualities in a single person, that person's love would only be a faint shadow of the furious love and mercy in the heart of God the Father addressed to you and me at this moment.

As warm (and unexpected) as the father's welcome was, the son had some confessing to do. It turned out to be his salvation.

And the son said to him, "Father, I have sinned against heaven and in your sight, and am no longer worthy to be called your son." But the father said to his servants, "Bring out the best robe and put it on him, and put a ring on his hand and sandals on his feet. And bring the fatted calf here and kill it, and let us eat and be merry; for this my son was dead and is alive again; he was lost and is found." And they began to be merry.

LUKE 15:21-24 NKJV

137

In the middle of the son's rehearsed plea to his father, the father interrupted his orphan speech! The father wouldn't let his son's religious prayer out of his mouth. Instead, he immediately turned to his servants and issued orders for his son's adornment. In so doing, he made a clear distinction between his servants and his son. *Look, boy, these are servants. You are not. You are mine, son, now and forevermore.*

Isn't this just like God's furious love? The Holy Spirit speaks straight to our identity—we are sons and daughters of Almighty God, now and forevermore.

> **In the middle of the son's rehearsed plea to his father, the father interrupted his orphan speech!**

The father's adornment of his son has symbolic importance for us today. The best robe he put on his son was most likely the father's robe, signifying a commissioning to forgive and restore. The signet ring on his son's finger signified restored trust with riches. The sandals on his feet were for the son's equipping so he could stand upright and walk with dignity.

Interestingly, the father's act of running toward the son could have had a secondary reason. The community knew the disgraceful act the son had committed. And so, in this culture, they had a right to mob him and beat him senseless. The father's embrace, while representing forgiveness, also demonstrated that if he forgave his son, the community also needed to forgive him.

When the father ordered the fatted calf to be prepared, it was not just to feed his sons and a few servants. This was a party, a community feast to celebrate that his son had returned home. It informed the community that the son was forgiven. It elevated him to a proper social status. The father was serving notice that his son wasn't merely returned, but that he was restored!

The fatted calf was a type of Christ. He is our redemption today.

Whoever eats My flesh and drinks My blood has eternal life, and I will raise him up at the last day.

JOHN 6:54 NKJV

You see, when we reconcile with the Father, it overflows to reconciliation with the people around us. When we discover the extravagant love of the Father, we cannot help but love and forgive all those around us.

When a man's ways please the Lord, He makes even his enemies to be at peace with him.

PROVERBS 16:7 NKJV

In this parable, Jesus was describing an extravagant love that broke cultural norms. The prodigal's father ran towards his son. Imagine the sound of the father's footsteps. That's a sound the son will never forget. He sees his father's face, feels his kisses of sweet forgiveness, and is embraced into life as he was meant to live—with the father.

> **We can't outrun the Father's pursuit of us and we can't outgrow our need for the Father's love!**

God pursues us down that same road as we return home. Can you hear it? It's the sound of relentless love pursuing us, a stampede of radical grace calling your name right now. We can't outrun the Father's pursuit of us and we can't outgrow our need for the Father's love!

My Beloved Sons

I have two sons of my own, David and Josiah. They are incredible young men: smart, anointed, and talented. I love them with all of my heart! It's hard to express how much I love my sons; nothing could change my love for them.

Recently, David was getting ready for a presentation to his college class. He emerged from his room in a sharp-looking suit. I looked at him with eyes of love, thinking how proud I am of him. Later, he told me his presentation went so well that his college professor bragged on his presentation in front of the class. The professor also elaborated on one of my son's points for twenty minutes. As my son was telling me this, I was thinking, *I am so stinkin' proud of you, Son!* That very moment, as I beheld my awesome son, the Holy Spirit stirred a fire deep within my heart. God had my attention! I heard the voice of my Abba so clearly: *If you look at your sons that way, imagine how proud I am of you, my beloved son.*

My heart melted; I thought of the voice of the Father resounding over Jesus.

> *And the Holy Spirit descended in bodily form like a dove upon him, and a voice came from heaven which said, "You are My beloved Son; in You I am well pleased."*
>
> LUKE 3:22 NKJV

Adopted by Abba

> *My identity as Abba's child is not an abstraction or a tap dance into religiosity. It is the core truth of my existence.*
> BRENNAN MANNING - *Abba's Child*

When I began in ministry, I was a prodigal son with orphan heart wounds. This had nothing to do with wandering away or, as many have experienced, life without a loving father. I was blessed with a loving father. If I could be half the dad my father was to me, I could raise 10,000 sons! Some people assume they have no orphan wounds because they grew up with a good dad, but the two are unrelated. My dilemma haunted me: *Why do I feel like an orphan as a Christian in ministry?*

I felt overlooked and invisible. I'd been rejected by pastors and leaders. Instead of allowing this to expand my heart, I grew distant. I was in ministry, doing great things, but still in a far country feeding pigs.

Even after years as a worship pastor and an associate pastor, I still carried these heart wounds. Then I met Larry M. Titus. He was scheduled to speak at our church, and when I picked him up from the airport, everything he spoke to me carried life and intention from a heart of love. His words were weighty with the substance of a father's love. It was simply who he was. My heart burned with a holy fire. I was astonished at the caliber of his anointing. I mean, this guy had an international ministry and had pastored mega-churches. Most astonishing, however, was that he talked to me as though he was interested in who I was. That never happened before.

> I was in ministry, doing great things, but still in a far country feeding pigs.

During his message to the congregation, he shared something that floored me. "I didn't just come to preach to you, but to adopt Zack."

Later, as he prayed over me, I felt the weight of orphan lies falling off of me. From that moment, Larry became a spiritual father to me.

A few years later, after we started the church in Las Vegas, Rachelle and I went to a conference with thousands of attendees, many of them pastors. I had been a senior pastor for a little over a year by then, and our church was thriving. We were excited to go and be refreshed as new pastors. Well, guess who one of the speakers was? Yep, Larry Titus. He delivered a powerful message, after which hundreds of pastors and leaders came to the altar in repentance.

After the ministry time, I walked up and said, "Hey Larry, I know you're busy, but we wanted to say hello." I would have been fine with a big-time man of God like him just acknowledging my existence, but Larry is so much more than that. He is a father. He is someone that the scandalous love of Father God flows through effortlessly.

Larry boomed: "I'm so glad to see you. I want to take you to lunch." I thought: *Why does he want to spend time with me?!* It may seem minor, but it was another healing breakthrough. *All these pastors much greater than I, and Larry wants to hang out with me?!*

I could have responded in false humility. "I'm not worthy to dine with you, oh man of God." Truth was, I wasn't going to miss this for the world!

I can't tell you what I ate or even where we went, but I'll never forget the love of the Father as Larry spoke into my life: "You're so awesome; I'm so proud of you." Those words didn't originate from Larry alone, but from the very heart of God.

A year after this, Larry invited me to a special pastoral gathering. It was a select group of twenty-four pastors from all over the world, ministers that he wanted to pour into for a few days. I was honored when Larry asked me to bring my guitar and be ready to lead worship.

Of course, as a worship pastor, I was used to leading worship gatherings, but Larry quickly corrected me. "Zack, I don't want you to just come and lead worship. You are one of the pastors I'm inviting. I want to pour into you."

Wow! My words caught in my throat as my eyes flooded. *What favor God is showing me!* I was humbled, honored, but mostly wrecked by the love of the Father. I turned toward home to see Dad running to me with an embrace and a kiss. I would never be the same.

The love, affirmation, discipleship, and fathering I have received from my spiritual father, Larry M. Titus, has made me who I am today. I could tell you so many stories of how his love has impacted me. To this day, Larry has always been there for me. I still can't believe he noticed me or actually answers my phone calls.

I was a senior pastor, broken like a prodigal son in a far country. I wasn't backslidden; I just needed a greater revelation of Abba's Love. When Larry said things like, "I'm so proud of you" or "I'm behind you 100 percent," I wasn't hearing a man's voice; it was the resounding voice of the Father.

Last Call

After all these pages, my message comes down to this. Prepare to hear the voice of God. Remove all distractions. Quiet your soul. Awaken your ears. Allow the Holy Spirit into your deepest being. Listen for Papa's whisper: "You are my beloved child, and I'm so proud of you."

> **I wasn't backslidden; I just needed a greater revelation of Abba's Love.**

Maybe it's the first time you've heard that message directly from the Father. It's that same voice that imparts new life as we are born again. That whisper sustains every heartbeat and every breath we breathe, even life itself.

> *If it were his [God's] intention*
> *and he withdrew his spirit and breath,*
> *all humanity would perish together*
> *and mankind would return to the dust.*
>
> JOB 34:14-15 NIV

To all the sons and daughters, the Father is saying: "I'm so proud of you! You're Daddy's kids, and that will never change!" Receive his love, his tender affection, and warm embrace. You will never be the same.

> *Look with wonder at the depth of the Father's marvelous love that he has lavished on us! He has called us and made us his very own beloved children.*
>
> 1 JOHN 3:1 TPT

When a newborn baby has an irregular heartbeat, nurses will lay the baby on the bare chest of the father, heart to heart. Not only does it keep the baby warm, but the father's heartbeat helps get the baby's heartbeat at a healthy rhythm.

Close your eyes right now and imagine you are resting on the heart of Papa God. Be still and breathe. There is no striving in love. Just be with him. There is healing in closeness to Abba. May your heart beat with his as the Holy Spirit works deep within.

God loves the broken world. God loves community. And God loves us . . . beyond our comprehension. Let us continue this journey into Abba's amazing love.

> **Imagine you are resting on the heart of Papa God. Be still and breathe. There is no striving in love.**

So I kneel humbly in awe before the Father of our Lord Jesus, the Messiah, the perfect Father of every father and child in heaven and on the earth. And I pray that he would unveil within you the unlimited riches of his glory and favor until supernatural strength floods your innermost being with his divine might and explosive power. Then, by constantly using your faith, the life of Christ will be released deep inside you, and the resting place of his love will become the very source and root of your life.

Ephesians 3:14-17 TPT

I wrote this book because I have been undone by the scandalous love of God. I pray you will be undone as well.

You are significant! Be loved. Be blessed!

At the close of this book, you might enjoy the song "Abba," sung by me, Zack Wechsler.

Reflection, Discussion, and Prayer

1. Based on what you learned in this chapter, describe the primary work of the Holy Spirit in your heart.

2. In Luke 15, Jesus revealed the extravagance of his Father's love. Ask the Holy Spirit to take away the old, wrong views of the Father and unveil how extravagant his love is towards you.

3. When the son came home, the father ran towards him. Reflect on how the Father has run toward you with love, forgiveness, and grace in different times of your life.

4. Think about how the Father has spoken to you and shown you love through others in your life. Can you hear him still speaking over you, "You are my beloved child, in whom my soul delights"? What else does the Father think about you?

IF YOU'RE A FAN OF THIS BOOK, WILL YOU HELP ME SPREAD THE WORD?

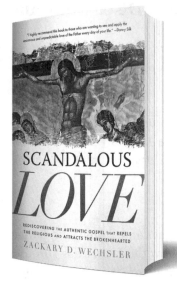

- There are several ways you can help me get the word out about the message of this book…
- Post a 5-Star review on Amazon.
- Write about the book on your Facebook, Twitter, Instagram, LinkedIn – any social media you regularly use!
- If you blog, consider referencing the book, or publishing an excerpt from the book with a link back to my website. You have my permission to do this as long as you provide proper credit and backlinks.
- Recommend the book to friends – word-of-mouth is still the most effective form of advertising.
- Purchase additional copies to give away as gifts.

The best way to connect with me is by going to my website: www.ScandalousLove.com

NEED A DYNAMIC SPEAKER
FOR YOUR NEXT EVENT?

www.ScandalousLove.com